D1058085

Of Africa

Of Africa

Wole Soyinka

Yale UNIVERSITY PRESS

New Haven and London

Yale University Press books may be purchased in quan-
tity for educational, business, or promotional use. For
information, please e-mail sales.press@yale.edu (U.S.
office) or sales@yaleup.co.uk (U.K. office).

Designed by Sonia Shannon.
Set in Garamond type by Integrated Publishing Solutions.
Printed in the United States of America.

Library of Congress Cataloging-in-Publication Data
Soyinka, Wole.
Of Africa / Wole Soyinka.
    p. cm.
    ISBN 978-0-300-14046-0 (cloth : alk. paper)
1. Africa—History. 2. Africa—Civilization. I. Title.
    DT20.S58 2012
    960—dc23   2012013544

A catalogue record for this book is available from the
British Library.

This paper meets the requirements of ANSI/NISO
Z39.48–1992 (Permanence of Paper).

10 9 8 7 6 5 4 3 2 1

Contents

Preface   vii

PART I   *Past into Present*

1. The Dark Continent? Or Beholder's Cataract?   3
2. Children of Herodotus   27
3. Fictioning of the Fourth Dimension   53
4. The Tree of Forgetfulness: Alive and Well in Darfur   67

PART II   *Body and Soul*

5. A Choice of Chains   93
6. Not a "Way of Life," But a Guide to Existence   104
7. The Spirituality of a Continent   129
8. Thus Spake Orunmila: Africa as Arbitrating Voice   169

Preface

What does the continent known as Africa possess that the rest—or a greater part—of the globe does not have already in superabundance? These, obviously, cannot be limited to material or inert possessions—such as mineral resources, touristic landscapes, strategic locations—not forgetting the continent's centuries-old designation as human hatcheries for the supply of cheap labor to other societies, East and West. There also exist dynamic possessions—ways of perceiving, responding, adapting, or simply *doing* that vary from people to people, including structures of human relationships. These all constitute potential commodities of exchange—not as negotiable as timber, petroleum, or uranium perhaps, but nonetheless recognizable as defining the human worth of any people—and could actually contribute to the resolution of the existential dilemma of distant communities, or indeed to global survival, if only they were known about or permitted their proper valuation.

There is also of course the aspect of negative attributes, one whose very nature constitutes a burden on others. We are speaking here of a condition where the unraveling of a part can menace the health or survival of the whole—a rather inglorious route to claims of significance, of demanding the attention of the rest. If we closed in just on Africa, ignoring the rest of the world for now, instability in the Congo or the Chad regions constitutes threats that must compel the continent not only to sit up and take notice, but to act preventively to stem the tide of destabilization outside the immediately affected borders. The barely resolved crisis in the oil-producing Delta region of Nigeria was a matter of global concern that spanned more than a decade. The same connectivity applies to the internal affairs of every nation across the globe. Just to shift parameters and direction, the once seemingly impregnable economies of Europe have become, in recent years, such zones of grave concern to the younger African nations, that Europe may be said to matter desperately to African nations in an unprecedented qualitative shift since colonialism and the initial phase of decolonization.

Ultimately, however, it is its humanity, the quality and valuation of its own existence, and modes of managing its environment—both physical and intangible (which includes the spiritual)—that remain the primary, incontestable assets to which any society can lay claim or offer as unique contributions to the attainments of the world. This interrogation constitutes our primary goal in its limited excursion into Africa's past and present.

For many, Africa is more a concept than a bounded space, which means, in turn: more "concepts" than simply one. It is at once part wish fulfillment and part reality, part projection and part historical distillation, part fiction and part memory. It is, of course, generally acknowledged as a warehouse of untapped natural resources. Even as Africa exists as a desire for some, so does it constitute a nightmare from which others pray to be awakened, a piece of history's tapestry whose threads can be unraveled without loss of definition to the rest. Yet many also appear eager to participate in this enticing but dubious banquet, convinced that Africa remains a space of infinite possibilities, one that only awaits its day of fulfillment. Of these, a fair number are resolved to be present at, and be part of, that event. This breed is ubiquitous. Immigration officers recognize them on sight. When they are pushed out of one gate they do not really live until they return through another. "I get expelled from Africa all the time," I have heard one such declare, suiting the familiar saying to his latest immigration bout, "but no one can expel Africa from within me."

These contending viewpoints do not belong to any specific groups—national, racial, religious, and so forth—nor are they mutually exclusive. We shall find Asians, Europeans, and Australians, progressives and reactionaries, capitalists and socialists, racists, idealists, investors, humanists, and technocrats espousing or repudiating one or all of these perspectives, and perhaps an equal number shifting grounds from one year to the next—it all depends on whether there has been another Rwanda, an underwear bomber from Nigeria, killer gas deposits in Lake Nyos productively tapped, or a new Nelson Mandela sprung to prominence in the slums of Malabo.

Africa—concept or reality—is an acknowledged continent of extremes, and, by the same token, it is hardly surprising that it draws extreme reactions. Africans themselves are just as divided in their responses or strategies of accommodation—acquiescing, protective, resigned or fiercely defensive, identifying with, justifying or dissociating themselves from what is apparent or presumed to lie beneath the surface. The in-

creasingly accepted common ground, both for the negativists and opti-
mists, is that the African continent does not exist in isolation, nor has it
stood still in a time warp, independent of history. On the contrary, the
continent is an intimate part of the histories of others, both cause and
consequence, a complex organism formed of its own internal pulsation
and external interventions, one that continues to be part of, yet is often
denied, the triumphs and advances of the rest of the world.

The contents of this book derive from a natural, sometimes frustrating preoccupation with this chameleonic entity, since it happens to be one
from whose definition, in general, I also derive mine. They revisit propositions encountered under widely different circumstances—university lecture halls, international conferences, roundtables, radio and television
programs. Some have proceeded from or have been shaped by, it must
also be admitted, the gamut of casual encounters in which the Africa
Phenomenon became an issue. These encompass magisterial, superior
attitudes such as, "But look here, let's face it, you must admit that there
is something of a problem about your peoples—look what's just happened in . . . / look at the scale of corruption in . . . /with just a fraction
of Africa's natural resources, compare . . ." These are sometimes pityingly
nuanced as invitations to the club of the exceptional breed from a zone
of dread and avoidance.

At the opposite end is the reassuring consensus on African traditional arts, all the way to optimistic, even enthusiastic prognosis for
her economy—"Africa is the next great economy to hit the world after
China, mark my words. Give it another twenty years and you'll see."—
all of which makes one wonder if we all apply the same development

yardsticks in assessing progress for such a vast continent. Then there are variations where an individual—an overnight notoriety or incorrigible ruler—is blithely conflated with the totality, so that one is expected to accept the brutality of one sadist or the clownery of another in international caucuses as proof of the savagery or imbecility of an entire continent. A sigh of relief should result when the subject turns to Africa's explosive soccer talent, virtually the only guaranteed zone of unforced, objective, (seemingly) knowledgeable pronouncements, but, alas, that is no solace to a nonenthusiast of that global pastime of mass hysteria.

There is one encounter, a quite recent one, that stands apart, an encounter which, in an ironic way, pushed even deeper the primary thrust of my partisanship, since the historic import of that incident appeared primed to undermine an antistereotypical conviction I have tried to render explicit on these pages. It took place in Bayreuth, Germany, in November 2009. I had referred, during the course of a lecture, to the controversy that took place a year earlier over the production of the opera *Idomeneo* by the Deutsche Oper (details in Chapter 8). Fears had been expressed about offending religious sensibilities through the opera's supposedly irreverent portrayal of religious avatars and prophets. In my address I pointed out that both Islam and Christianity had been guilty not merely of physical atrocities on African soil, including enslavement of the indigenes, but of a systematic assault on African spirituality in their contest for religious hegemony. Therefore the claims of either religion to mutual tolerance, I proposed, were still limited to the binary insularity of the world's incorrigible hegemonists, since they have proved incapable of taking into consideration the rights of other religions to equal respect, equal space, and tolerance. Still—as frankly championed between these covers—I offered that, for that very reason, those "invisible" religions of the world occupied a unique position to act as neutral arbiters whenever the two rivals went for each other's throats.

At the dinner that followed, an interjection that this elicited from a young man, perhaps thirty years of age, proved to have implications far beyond the scope of my speculative intent. Its offensiveness was trivial; more critical was its indication of a deeply embraced credo—not just for that individual but for an absent ideological coterie whose views he had only articulated. I heard not one voice but many, from across Europe and other continents. Usually suppressed, it nonetheless only awaited a chance to burst forth—and not merely in abrasive words across a dinner table, but in organized bouts of xenophobic violence. His remarks went thus:

> Africans, you must admit, are inherently inferior. You must
> be, or other races would not have enslaved you for centuries.
> Your enslavers saw you for what you were, so you cannot
> blame them.

It was that stark, delivered with precision, like a well-rehearsed position statement. The table—at least the portion within hearing—fell quiet. With equal quietness I transferred to another place at the table. A few moments later the young interlocutor also left, unannounced.

"The good, the bad, and the ugly," a popular Nigerian columnist once sighed in a fit of frustration over the improbable nation into which he had been born without—he protested—any prior consultation! The title of that spaghetti Western often appears to have been tailored for the entire continent, but then, is that not the realistic condition even of the most advanced of Western and Asian nations, even without such portents as the incident I have just narrated? Our exposition makes a point of keeping this constantly at the foreground of facile, generalized summations of a diverse continent and its peoples. At base, however, and of greater interest to this contribution than one revelation of racist indoctrination, or indeed effusive eulogies, it proposes, very simply, that History has erred. All claims that Africa has been explored are as premature as news of her imminent demise. A truly illuminating exploration of Africa has yet to take place. It does not pretend to take place even on the pages of this book, whose scope is limited to retrieving a few grains for germination from the wasteful threshing floor of Africa's existential totality. One hopes they will sprout a new breed of explorers for the relay race toward a deeply craved Age of Universal Understanding—Africa inspired.

PART I *Past into Present*

I.   The Dark Continent? Or Beholder's Cataract?

> The euphoria and optimism that accompanied the indepen-
> dence of African nations have evaporated, often in the most
> brutal manner, leaving the continent not only in a situation
> of unprecedented poverty but also [in] a frightening level of
> socio-economic decay.
>
> Millennium Commission report, 2001

THUS COMMENCES THE PREAMBLE to the document that emerged from
a brainstorming caravan launched by the former secretary-general of
the United Nations, Kofi Annan, in collaboration with Professor Albert
Tedjevore of the Republic of Benin. Its visitations lasted over a year and
traveled through several African capitals, culminating in the capital of
Ivory Coast, Abidjan, under the hospitality of its head of state, Laurent
Gbagbo. With an unwelcome fortuitousness, that nation has leapt to
the fore as a sobering exemplar of the deep malaise that continues to
eviscerate the African continent—and from within.

"Such initiatives are not new," warn the authors of the Millennium document, listing a number of its predecessors and stressing their intention to build on past efforts: "The Commission has taken note of other efforts such as the Lagos Plan of Action, the Arusha Declaration, UNESCO's Audience Africa, MAP, OMEGA, plus a number of other encounters, some of which have crystallized into The New Partnership for Africa's Development (NEPAD), whose principles were adopted by African Heads of State at Lusaka."

The participants were under no illusion that a magical transformation would result from their labors—if anything, they were prey to the discouraging legacy of repetitiousness and to a niggling warning of futility. Nonetheless, it is in the nature of hope that some events, especially attainments that constitute a measure of advance, nudge us toward an assessment that amounts to a quantifiable breakthrough from a state of stagnation or, indeed, from a reversal of a history of retrogression, such assessments attaining even hyperbolic dimensions. Certainly, in some circles of African leadership, they promoted the annunciation of a Renaissance long before its advent. Principal among such achievements would definitely rank the seeming miracle of South Africa, where the dead weight of the past on the umbilical cord of a fragile birth—majority rule—was exorcized in a manner that took even the most optimistic of the entire world by surprise. Even more recent was the resolution of the decades-old conflict in the Sudan. It was the former, however, that impressed upon the world a unique lesson on the possible routes to the resolution of seemingly intractable conflicts.

Africa appears doomed to oscillate between the polarities of hope and despair, a condition that is perhaps best illustrated by two events, two variations on one theme in stark contrast to each other and a true reflection of the realities of a continent. One took place in a subdued, quite minor key, far more deserving of exposure than was accorded it and still lacking in popular awareness in most parts of the continent till today. I refer to the parturition of a new voice for the continent, an independent communication and information access across borders, one that would operate resolutely outside governmental control even though powered by governmental will, in partnership with the Open Society Initiative for West Africa, and—to some extent—sustained by governmental resources. With an infectious confidence in its permanence, it was named West African Democracy Radio. Launched in August 2005, not long after the cessation of the serial bloodletting in Liberia, that seemingly interminable phase of negativity was ultimately sealed off with the election of the first-ever female president of an African nation, who, in 2011, was awarded the Nobel Prize for Peace. It was this affirmation of confidence in the resolution of that protracted war that made it possible for such a leader, Ellen Johnson-Sirleaf, together with three other West African heads of state—a loose consortium of the Mano River Basin States—to launch such a potent symbol and role-player in the quest for inclusive governance on the continent.

The launch took place in Dakar, Senegal, when four democratically elected leaders committed to the mission of giving permanence to a potent tool of democracy on a continent that both European and African voices had declared, when and as convenient—which was almost all the time—historically and temperamentally unsuited to the democratic option of governance. Unfortunately, at the very last moment, the new

Liberian president could not attend. She sent a representative, however, and, through her, a message which, despite its banter, encapsulated much of Africa's contemporary travails even as it constituted a challenge to the host country, Senegal, as well as the other partners in that venture.

The radio station had been conceived several years before, and its original home should have been Monrovia, capital of Liberia. The civil war prevented the actualization of that dream. In her message, President Johnson-Sirleaf regretted that the station had to be installed outside her own country, adding, tongue-in-cheek, that if ever the Senegalese government wearied of the presence of that democratic voice on its soil, Liberia was more than ready to resume her original designation as host. Delivered, as it was meant, as a tease between colleagues, the message signaled for all who were present a genuine turning point, a note of optimism, a symbol and portent for the future of a continent.

Assailing the minds of more than a handful of those present on that occasion must have been memories of the other event, the twinned potential of that communication facility whose Rwandan version was the very antithesis of the Mano River Basin collaboration. Radio Mille Collines of Rwanda, the instrument of that other polarity, was used with a brutal efficacy that resulted in the massacre of three quarters of a million people in under three weeks. After such a depressing recollection, and a succession of allied news of harrowing dimensions in one corner of Africa after another, the Mano occasion was a bracing augury. And then, as if to expunge the toxicity of the past years, and to set a seal on the full import of this collaboration between four leaders, news emerged of the arrest of the warlord Charles Taylor, butcher of Liberia and, later, her president. Taylor was packaged to the Hague to stand trial for crimes against humanity, encouraging the people of the West African subregion to hope that this was indeed the end of a nightmare, and that it signaled the end of the toleration of leadership impunity, a deterrent to other alienated leaders of a continent.

Would it? Taylor's arrest took place, after all, after the lesson of the pitiable, sadistic end of his predecessor Sergeant Doe—literally killed piecemeal, forced to drink a child's urine. It did not appear to have served as a lesson for Charles Taylor, not even after he had climbed to power on the rickety rungs of a war-weary democratic ladder. His rule went beyond accustomed brutality and, in any case, so deeply mired in blood was the path of his ascent that the opposition forces could not be expected to acquiesce for long in his leadership. The collective memory of victims of his "loyal subjects" pronounced his very presence a mockery of political legitimacy.

And then, Ivory Coast! Was the earlier debacle of the Ivory Coast in 2002 unexpected? Of course not! If anything, it was predicted! Even if, as the participants gathered in Abidjan for the Millennial Commission, they had been totally ignorant of the discontent that simmered beneath the surface, once they had set foot on the soil of Ivory Coast very few were long denied knowledge of the fact that this futuristic conference had been plunged right into a cauldron from the past. The so-called democracy of Ivory Coast was a sham. For decades that nation, under Felix Houphouet-Boigny, was lauded as a model of positive development and stable democracy. Yet it was nothing more than a patriarchal one-party dictatorship whose political success was built upon the very principle of exclusion, masquerading under the seemingly innocuous label of *ivoirité*. The outsider may be forgiven for thinking that *ivoirité* was an expression of nationalism—Cote d'Ivoire by Ivorians for Ivorians (as opposed to "for the French," etc.)—but the Ivorians knew better.

The wealth of Ivory Coast, its very success in self-reliance, was built on the labor of such so-called foreigners, and—important to note—these "foreigners" were fellow West Africans from neighboring countries, most notably from Burkina Faso (formerly Upper Volta). A large number of these "immigrants" had lived in Ivory Coast for generations, occupied high-level positions—governmental and political, including premiership—carried Ivorian passports, and neither knew any other country nor claimed any other nationality. Yet, purely for reasons of convenient electoral numbers, they were excluded from exercising their voice in the very land that had achieved its economic reputation from their sweat. This was a boil that was set to burst, and burst it did! Member states of the West African subregion in particular must have found the Ivory Coast eruption especially excruciating, given the fact that their concerted efforts had just begun to stabilize two other members—Liberia and then Sierra Leone—whose internecine conflicts had cost that region unquantifiable lives and resources, not to mention the ethical ruination of a young generation, a generation that grew up as child soldiers with a catalogue of atrocities behind them. Those atrocities were of a nature that would surely have landed the perpetrators, were they older, in the international tribunals for crimes against humanity.

We shall insist, however, on placing the African continent in a global context, so let us note that the problem of exclusivity is not peculiar to the African continent. The European, American, and Asian worlds, the Middle East—all the way southward to Australasia—are themselves riddled with the affliction. Can one ever forget the deployment of the Australian navy to ward off from its shores a boatload of fugitives from the Talibanic scourge? The rise of extreme nationalism, often developing into outright xenophobia, barely disguised under legislative formalisms that never name their real goal—exclusion—is a symptom of the increase, not decrease, of the we-or-they mentality that appears to be sweeping across the globe. It has resulted in wars of varying degrees of bloodiness and duration, of which perhaps the most notorious was the prolonged low-intensity yet vicious Irish civil war that appears at long last to be in genuine remission, despite violent instances of recidivism occurring as recently as 2009. The final decommissioning of weapons in that murder arena took place, significantly, under the supervision of an African statesman—Cyril Ramaphosa. Even more bloodied and exclusionist were the ethnic cleansing fields of Bosnia-Herzegovina, which eventually forced the North Atlantic Treaty Organization into armed intervention. These are wars whose roots, however traceable to histories of repression and competition for resources, are nonetheless products of the exclusivist narrowness of vision among peoples, and Africa cannot be held to be exceptional.

However, the diary of conflicts of exclusion that closed the twentieth century for Africa and launched the twenty-first—in Liberia, Ivory Coast, Congo, Rwanda, etc.—makes that continent a case for extreme concern and urgent strategies, even as the Bosnian eruption was recognized, almost belatedly, as a challenge to modern Europe. It is for this reason that the dismal example offered by Ivory Coast—with its complication of broad divisions between the north (Islamic) and south (Christian)—in the repeated negation of the Renaissance dream comes in so handily to illustrate the foundational flaw in the edifice of the African nation-state, and the role that a strict adherence to democratic justice must play in cementing the cracks in such an edifice.

Allied to exclusivity is another bugbear of a continent: boundaries. Boundaries imply exclusion, and it is undeniable that this tainted seed of guaranteed future conflicts on the continent was sown at the infamous Berlin Conference of 1884. It was there that Africa, a continent of so many cultures, precolonial trade patterns, and development traditions, was shared piecemeal among the western powers, with no consideration for their histories, languages, and economic linkages. What African leaders have so far failed to tackle in a systematic way is this: What are the consequences of this quilt work? Again, that is a question whose answer demands of leadership a very special kind of courage— moral and self-sacrificial: the readiness to yield divisions of power and control, if needed. Africa has never herself delineated her constituent national boundaries, those boundaries being humiliatingly inflicted on her by others. Is it really possible to deny the origins of some of her internecine conflicts to that carving out in the history of the continent? If the probability, at the very least, exists, is it then unthinkable that other conflicts presently "in denial," and perhaps of far more catastrophic potential for the continent, will erupt even as the present ones—Congo, the Sudan, Ethiopia, etc.—are doused?

Nations are not merely multicolored patches in the atlas, they answer to some internal logic and historic coherence, and an evolved tradition of managing incompatibilities. We all know the history of Eritrea and Ethiopia long before the intrusion of the colonial powers—largely Italy and Britain. We know how the foundations of present-day Liberia were laid. Those periods differ drastically from today's realities of international politics, commerce, and, indeed, the trend toward what is now called globalization. The hard questions are not being asked: In the context of present realities, are those national entities on the continent still viable? Is there cause for their reexamination?

Now, when such questions are posed, there is a tendency to suggest that one is already implying one answer, and one answer only—the disintegration of the present national entities, accompanied or unaccompanied by a reversion to the precolonial conditions of the rudimentary state. I have always found this response an unnecessarily negative preconditioning. Why should such an exercise not result in its opposite, the amalgamation of existing national entities? One response to this might be that it has been tried unsuccessfully—the Ghana-Guinea-Mali federation, or the Egyptian-Libyan shotgun marriage that was never consummated. Yet the fact that such projects recorded failures in the sixties does not mean that they will do so in the vastly changed socioeconomic realities of the twenty-first century.

By the same token—that is, for the reason of these very changes—one must concede that such a project of boundary reconsideration could end in just another debacle. It is clear, therefore, that engagement in such an exercise, even if only theoretically, arises because some of the current civil conflicts—such as that of the Sudan—are legitimately traceable to a fusion that was forced upon peoples, not one that proceeded from their political will and self-ordering. Where this is seen clearly to be the case, and internal instability of a costly dimension evidently derives from such impositions, common sense urges that, at the very least, the basis for such amalgamations be revisited with a view to ascertaining where precisely lies the will of the people themselves, acting in freedom. The Ethiopia-Eritrea fires, no sooner doused than threatening new flare-ups—even as recently as 2008—indicate that there is unfinished business in the functionality of those boundaries that African leadership and the rest of the world treat as sacrosanct. The consequences of refugee flow on the economy of African nations, even the most internally stable nations, can no longer be ignored. It had already escalated beyond manageable proportions in the upheavals of the final decades of the last century. And now Darfur has brutally challenged a continent in a way that it has not been challenged since the genocide of Rwanda. Taken together with the thirty-year civil war in southern Sudan that has even more rigorously questioned the primacy of boundaries in political association, the boundary factor has yet again manifested itself as a candidate for new positioning.

There is indeed one unsuspected benefit in the pursuit of this exercise, were it to be undertaken. It is contingent upon and will surely lead to a reexamination of the problem of exclusivity. In considering what the imperial powers chose to include within or exclude from the artificial nations that were created, African leaders may come to ask why. Why was this distinct nationality, and not that other, included in or excluded from a current nation space? The circumstantial answers should not interest us—such as treaties signed with a local chieftain, the arrival of one nation's exploration party seconds ahead of another, or the planting of an imperial flag. Of more relevant interest is one factor that is common to all such appropriations of other people's lands and resources: self-interest.

Africa's self-interest? Is it truly in the interest of the occupants of that continent that the present boundaries are being consolidated, defended, held so inviolate that the population is routinely decimated, millions maimed and incapacitated for life, vast hectares of farmland rendered useless by liberally sown antipersonnel mines? Once unheard-of diseases have now become daily currency—AIDS at a most alarming rate—robbing entire villages of their adult population as the dogs of war carry its virus across zones of conflict and even into neighboring nations at peace. Youths are robbed of their innocence and their human-ity as the continent becomes the corrupted playground of boy soldiers. In short, what price is worth paying for the illusion of boundaries and "sovereignty"? In what order of priorities is placed the interest of the people who inhabit the continent over whose spoils aliens have fought and still fight both directly or through surrogates—the surrogates being, alas, Africans themselves, their leadership selectively targeted? And what characterizes these surrogates? What makes them available in the first place and guarantees the ease of their replacement once their usefulness is expended?

The honeypot of power, to begin with. Power, as was demonstrated in the driving motivation of General Guei, invited into power as arbiter in the Ivorian crisis in 1999, but who turned electoral manipulator for his dictatorial ambitions. The habitually understated factor of the lust for power that needs a bounded estate to manifest itself is indeed a root cause of conflicts that are routinely deemed ethnic or religious. Such conflicts owe their genesis to the fundamental obsession with political supremacy and, of course, control of a nation's resources—preferably to the exclusion of others. They may indeed take on an ethnic or religious coloration as the contestants lose all scruples, co-opt, and manipulate the guileless and calculating alike into their ranks, playing on emotive issues that are falsely premised. To make matters worse, foreign powers and transnational corporations loved to deal with dictatorships—contracts are signed much more quickly, with less institutional overseeing, and it is in the interest of the dictator to help the foreigners "keep the natives in order" while the wealth of the nation is siphoned out, the land is degraded through mineral exploration, eternal gas flares from petroleum destroy fauna and environment, traditional fishing ponds are polluted, the birds drop dead from the air while toxic and pulmonary diseases sap the vitality of the people. Thus enters the rationalization of both military takeovers and their mimic one-party democracies, through recourse to a fictional African past. Democracy, they fictionalize, is foreign to African traditions. The mythology of the "strongman" as a necessity for bringing the continent into the mainstream of a modern world becomes the gospel of trading missions, designating the committed democrats infidels and apostates.

We must not, however, dismiss or underestimate the role of ideology—the genuine article this time—in Africa's predicament, even if today we appear to have moved beyond the heady, often mindless partisanships of the Cold War. While that ideological contest lasted, Africa was a plaything in the hands of both communist and capitalist ideological realms, or, more accurately, between the blocs that carried the banner of one ideology or the other. This was a season—the sixties, seventies, and eighties of the last century—when ideology became an abstraction, a rarefied zone that seduced some of the best minds on the continent—quite understandably, especially for the ideologues of the Left. However, it led to the frittering away of their productive energies on behalf of alien interests that took no notice of the material conditions of the societies over which they sought to spread the ideological banners—of both contesting hues. The intelligentsia also played into the hands of leadership, who were thus enabled to camouflage agendas of raw, naked power under the authority of radical/progressive or religious ideological adhesion. Demand of Mathieu Kerekou of the Republic of Benin, for instance, what he understood of Marxism when he woke up one morning and declared his nation a Marxist state. Or of Chiluba what he ate the night before he declared Zambia a Christian state. Or of Ahmed Yerimah, then governor of Zamfara State in Nigeria, what revelation he had when, long before his exposure as a serial pedophile, he pronounced his state—within a secular constitution—a Moslem state, to be henceforth administered according to the sharia. These are individuals to whom a space of governance is a mere playground, no different from a golf course or a gambling casino.

To these, and their external controllers, Africa evidently matters—but uniformly for the wrong reasons. While they toyed with the lives of millions, deviations from alien prescriptions—secular or theocratic—

for governance and economic responsibilities for African society became crimes of life and death, and societies stagnated under numerous shades of ideological purism. We have only to recall the example of Sékou Touré of the Republic of Guinea, a once admired revolutionary and pan-Africanist, and his infamous torture chambers, compared to which the Cameroonian Ahidjo's own chambers and concentration camps seemed closer to boy scout sadism. The much favored of Sékou Touré's instruments of persuasion were diabolical electric boxes whose existence many passionate and sincere progressives continued to deny as fabrications of western imperialist enemies of progress, until confronted with the stark evidence after his death. Under the remorseless run of a radical pan-Africanism and a Marxist theology, even the first secretary-general of the OAU, Diallo Telli, was not spared, and perished miserably in prison.

There are of course several models of exclusion and methods of executing such policies, some of them more blatant than the nominal distinction between citizens of one West African country and another. In 2009, the exclusionist determination led to one of the most vicious interethnic uprisings of Kenyan history—Luo versus Gikuyu and their subsidiary allies—which seared the sensibilities of the most hardened Africans, still numbed by the Rwandan massacres.

Then, sometimes, racial categorization is at issue. Failure to objectivize the problem of identity—racial identity—has been, all too often, the consequence of ideological posturing. It has led to avoidance, a leadership coyness that has left—at the very least—a specific genre of conflict unchecked. The first-line ideologues of African liberation loved to persuade themselves that, once the class conflict—which they had also bound with anti-imperialism and decolonization—was resolved, the issue of identity would vanish from the face of the earth, and of Africa most especially. It happened in the United States also, during the Black liberation struggle of the sixties and seventies. Take the African-American nationalists—in and out of their flirtation with Marxism and black nationalism. When, in the latter phase, they insisted that race, as the issue of the twentieth century, was not a prediction that had died with W. E. B. Du Bois, they were vilified by the "race-blind" ideologues—they were revisionists, petit-bourgeois intellectuals, primitivists, even racists. South Africa's ANC, anxious to build a classless, colorblind society as a counter to the hideous travesties of the racist ideology of Apartheid, anxious to distance itself completely from that antihumanistic creed, equally attempted to wish race away.

The consequence—and we are not attempting here to negate or diminish the lofty idealism of that liberation "rainbow" catechism, very much the contrary—the consequence, however, is simply that the problem is still actively with us, resulting in amoral muteness toward zones of race-defined conflict. It is often difficult to understand and explain why leading progressive voices, even within South Africa and her race experience, remain silent or are apologetic over the race inspired policies of the Sudanese government. The result? Having denied, in a textbook-bound phase, that race can be a factor in any struggle, having transcended race, under "enlightened," "progressive," "radical" conviction, it becomes difficult to objectively accept its eruption as a fatal factor in internal governance even of blatantly racist regimes. (More of this in Chapter 4.) The outcome, however, stares the continent in the face, and that outcome is the racial cleansing of a vast tract of human space within Sudan, the expulsion of thriving strings of communities from their homeland, in figures that are now reckoned in millions. We are speaking here of massacres and rape—in short, the dehumanization of a people who are identified by race in history, in internal ruling classification, and by attestation. We can of course take refuge in the exercise of debating comparative weights of the reasons for this predicament. We already know of a major and certainly predominant one—the discovery of natural resources, oil to be specific. But it castrates one's intellect, and limits options for resolution, to ignore any determinant base or contributory factor, such as the identity of those who have been collectively brutalized, and one incontrovertible factor is: they are black African peoples, the indigenous occupants of that tract of land, marked by a history of a slaving relationship and thus assigned a subhuman status in the eyes of a ruling elite of Arab attestation.

Can the African continent truly afford the luxury of glossing history or sweeping its painful lessons under the carpet in an endeavor to enter mainstream world acceptance, especially of the "progressive," "radical" affirmation? If the history of the African peoples has no significance, then the continent's present claims to existence are sham and do not matter to anyone.

Fortunately, Africa is much grander than the sum of her politics—even of the most progressive tenor. Before turning one's face to the wall, the continent of which it has been said "there is always something new out of" has indeed a history and present of surprises that not only extend our concept of human creativity but illuminate many conundrums of human existence and destination. The humanism preached by poets and writers, of whom the poet-statesman Léopold Sédar Senghor was prime promoter, remains a generous though largely obscured reality. Senghor placed this humanism at the foundation of his conceptual edifice of Negritude—the being of blackness, among other definitions. Yet it was a concept that advanced beyond racial separatism to propose the eventuality of a universal synthesis of humanistic values, and it stimulated deeper explorations and creative animation of the cultures that housed those values long before the iconoclastic collusion (and rivalries) of east and west, Islam and Christianity, for the negation of African self-esteem. Senghor's agenda for the African presence was straightforward:

> The problem we blacks now face is to discover how we are going to integrate African Negro values into the world of 1959. It is not a question of resuscitating the past, of living in an African Negro museum; it is a question of animating the world, here and now, with the values of the past.
> *(2nd Congress of African Writers and Artists, Rome, 1959)*

At the core of Senghor's vision, shared by authoritative voices from a different calling, such as Archbishop Desmond Tutu, is that yet untapped resource of African humanism, so deeply lodged within her spirituality, one that goes by many names—Tutu refers to it as *ubuntu,* a South African word that he translates as "the bundle of humanity." The continent has continued to quarry inward, then reached outward in the attempt to render palpable what must always be found as an elusive extract, one, however, that may hold a key to the "Renaissance" that is so tantalizingly projected on a receding horizon. That essence may ensure that, indifferent to the indifference of the world, Africa profoundly matters to her own— and for reasons that are not only laudable but universally applicable.

The export of symbols, or essences, when their reality is so sorely needed on home ground, may sometimes appear like the agenda of Esu (the Yoruba god of contradictions)—or Tantalus—in operation on a continent. Yet there is a sense of ancestral splendor in the fulfillment of an unwitting, prophetic summons by our priest of the gospel of *civilisation universelle,* Senghor, a possessed griot who squinted at columns of steel and chrome-tinted glass in a city that narrated the chronicle of western separatism and its gleaming sterility, and launched an exhortation, separated only by lyrical tonalities from that of Martin Luther King Jr.'s "I have a dream." Senghor little dreamt that this exhortation would be made flesh, and in a most spectacular feat of timing and magnitude—the election of an African descendant to power in the United States—when he sang:

> New York, I say New York, let the black blood flow into
> your veins
> Cleaning the rust from your steel articulations, like an oil
> of life . . . !

A convenient moment, however, to pause and address this question: What is Africa? What does the term consist of? A mere geographical expression, as a Nigerian statesman once said of that former British colony, Nigeria? The habitation, *simplicitas,* of a people who consider and address themselves as Africans? The homeland of a race loosely defined as black, with certain attributes of skin, hair, and distinct physiognomy? The predatory ground for a steady supply of forced labor for over two millennia? To many of course the problem does not exist. They are conditioned to the straightforward saline solution—the continent that is washed by the Atlantic Ocean to the west, the Indian Ocean to the east, and the Mediterranean Sea to the north. Yet within that landmass live people who also consider themselves Arabs and identify historically, culturally, politically, and religiously with the conglomerate known as the Arab world, and in whose perception those other self-cognizing Africans belong to a race of otherness.

This lack of precision—or clamor of multiple definitions—has not, however, prevented (it perhaps even encouraged) generations displaced over centuries from identifying emotionally, culturally, and programmatically with what is seen as ancestral origin, even going beyond this to embark on strategies of formal recognition, despite centuries of absence and the most tenuous linkages—or none at all—to the continent. The event of the ascension of an "African" or "black" person to the presidency of the United States, home to millions of displaced Africans, has, not surprisingly, contributed to an upsurge of assertions of such racial/national identity claims in the least expected places, places where, until now, there had been assumptions of a unified national—and race-blind— identity. This hardly induces much optimism for the abandonment or diminution in the consciousness of racial distinctions. If you insist that you are a distinct, separate entity in refutation of what, hitherto, had been generally accepted as a homogenous identity with others, you are already creating a new, distinct axis of self-perception. One could point, for instance, to the Sudan, but we need not even go for that notorious state of governmental alienation and routine morbidity, where the language of racism has unleashed one of the most brutal internal suppressions of a civilian entity in contemporary times. Let us employ instead the more benign Iraq as instruction. The word "benign," applied to Iraq, must sound near blasphemous, but no, the reference here is to a quite recent and peaceful phenomenon.

The Iraqi grid-work of identities that the world knew of—and to a large extent still does—was composed of the Shi'ites, the Sunnis, and the Kurds. Suddenly news emerged that an Afro-Iraqi population not only exists but now insists on being recognized and designated as a distinct African minority. Students of history have of course known this for much longer. They learned that an African group of rebellious slaves from the salt mines took over a swathe of the valley of the Euphrates in the ninth century, set up an independent territory, and resisted all efforts at reconquest for over fifteen years. In other words, the very earliest sustained black slave uprising and autonomous governance in history took place a full millennium before the Americas or the West Indies, Haiti being perhaps the best known, since it resulted in the enthronement of a black republic after the defeat of the army of a powerful European slaving nation—France.

Ralph Ellison's classic *The Invisible Man,* a work most generous for extraction of metaphors of race and identity, could very well have been set, and perhaps even more dramatically, in Iraq, or in several North African and Middle Eastern countries, from Morocco to Iran. The world of historians and cultural sociology has displayed a remarkable level of disinterestedness in these obscured realities of the African past and present. The eventual emergence of an African identity assertion from within Iraq was of course enabled—first by the fall of Saddam Hussein and the fragmentation of that country following the Iraqi war, and, next, by the sweeping transformation of minds and outlook in the faraway nation (leading to the election of her first president of African descent) of the United States, which had brought about Iraq's fragmentation in the first place. So, what does it mean for the world? What does it mean that the voiceless are suddenly given voice, that the invisible suddenly take form, voice, and numbers but above all seek to reintegrate themselves into certain values, a recourse of which they remain uncertain, beyond the fact that the world has systematically denied, degraded, or suppressed those values.

The negative prospect is obvious: an internal restlessness within repressive regimes with a will to homogenization. To all such—especially in matters of religion—plurality is prelude to disruptiveness and a weakening of centralist control, not to be tolerated.

The optimistic answer has already been inserted, as rhapsodized by our elected griot, Léopold Sédar Senghor. To him and his fellow visionaries—Aimé Césaire, Nicolás Guillén, Léon Damas, Cheikh Anta Diop, and others—Africa, spread from the continent itself, westward to Europe and the Americas, eastward to the Indian continent, the deserts of Arabia, and the historic waters of the Euphrates, that yet denied Af-

rica pulsates as the potential leaven in the exhausted dough of the world.
A potential leaven that is without risks of the exercise of an imperialist
will that has so massively bedeviled the encounter between Africa and
the rest of the world.

For, in answering that earlier question, unanswerable even as it was
phrased—what is Africa?—one certain response, definitely in the negative, is: *not* a hegemonic construct, nor one that aspires to be. The history
of Africa places her outside the contending hegemonies of the world,
which perhaps is why a certain school of historicism, supposedly progressive, once insisted that Africa has been placed outside world history.
This hegemonic temper will be not be found in any field of human
endeavor, certainly not in the religious nor in the cultural. Africa may
have captured the imagination of schools of artistic representation from
time to time, most notably toward the closing of the nineteenth and
the first decades of the twentieth centuries in Europe, but there it ended.
It did not attempt to dictate or disseminate her artistic traditions or
prohibitions—contrast this with some religions—in any hegemonic
manner, but left the temperaments of national and international artists
to find within her treasure house whatever they sought for their own
creative fulfillment. Not even in dress fashion, nor in culinary choices—
again, contrast this with some religions—did the continent known as Africa attempt impositions on other parts of the world, though of course
these played their role in the liberation of the African-American psyche
from the stranglehold of Euro-American givens. In religion most especially, despite spreading her spirituality to the Americas and the Caribbean on the shackles of slavery—a condition that did not stem from

their own volition—African religions did not aspire to conquer the world. If anything they were reticent, but they proved resilient. It offers a new interpretation to that cry of Aimé Césaire, Léopold Sédar Senghor's spiritual sibling whose Negritude passion even led to a rhapsody of denial: "Hurrah for those who never invented anything." That was of course a hyperbolism that attracted indignant repudiation even from some of his associates in the Negritude movement. In retrospect, and in a special context, a revisionist exercise might make Césaire's rhapsody prescient after all, for hegemony implicates domination in fields of human achievement, and this may be one of those instances where the hegemonic lack pays off, where, in fact, it suddenly helps to have been "invisible" in history, thus posing no threat to established world rivalries in their contention for dominance. Put simply: politically, technologically, commercially, and in religion, Africa has never posed a hegemonic threat. Where such motions have taken off geographically, Africa—north of the Sahara—has merely served as a springboard for invaders and conquerors to whom that portion of Africa had itself succumbed in prolonged vassalage. In the provenance of religion, one that has now shot to the top as the world's most active destabilizing agent, so remote from any notion of religious hegemonism has the continent been uniformly deemed, that the entire vastness of that peopled land was even pronounced to be beyond the sheerest sensibilities of the spiritual in man. No wonder the continent has lately become yet again the warring ground of the world's traditional hegemonists (albeit tied to the politics and economic pursuits of their religious proponents).

To that world of the supremacist urge belongs the privilege of choice, informed by a frank assessment of its past relationship with the continent and her offerings. "Invisibility" is not quite the same as immateriality or a void of values, intangible or palpable. Today's global reality is one of acute polarization, like the globe itself and the invisible poles on which it spins. Solutions to the binary contestation for space for the domination of ideas can come only from alternative worlds that remain outside the affiliations of such polarities, albeit increasingly subjected to their pressure, demanding partisanship. Precolonial Africa—which still sustains the subterranean reality of the African authentic being—has survived the violence of centuries and the sometimes prolonged disruption of its organic strategies of existence. The value of Africa to the world remains its untapped source—but source for what? As an "invisible continent"— invisible as in Ellison's parable of invisibility—populated solely by much coveted inert, material assets? Or, alternatively, as a humanized resource for continuing self-transformation that will place an enlightened face on a renewed Scramble for Africa.

First, however, that external world must come to terms with a tradition of self-indulgence that encouraged layers of visual cataract to accumulate and harden over centuries, obscuring a truthful apprehension of the continent. The darkness that was so readily attributed to the "Dark Continent" may yet prove to be nothing but the willful cataract in the eye of the beholder.

2. Children of Herodotus

THE AFRICAN CONTINENT APPEARS TO possess one distinction that is largely unremarked. Unlike the Americas or Australasia, for instance, no one actually claims to have "discovered" Africa. Neither the continent as an entity nor indeed any of her later offspring—the modern states—celebrates the equivalent of America's Columbus Day. This gives it a self-constitutive identity, an unstated autochthony that is denied other continents and subcontinents. The narrative history of encounters with Africa does not dispute with others or revise itself over the "discovery" of Africa. Even her name is not attached to any enterprising nation, power, or individual adventurer. Africa appears to have been "known about," speculated over, explored both in actuality and fantasy, even mapped—Greeks, Jews, Arabs, Phoenicians, etc., took their turns—but no narrative has come down to us that actually lays personal or racial claim to the discovery of the continent. Ancient ruins, the source of a river, mountain peaks, exotic kingdoms, and sunken pyramids, yes, but not the continent itself—as in the case of the Americas. Hundreds have ventured into, explored, and extensively theorized over the continent, but no one has actually claimed to have discovered her.

Is this to be considered a badge of honor, a certificate of universal validation, or is there a hidden denigration somewhere? A vast continent, and not worth "discovering"? One could claim that it lends her an aura of the primordial, a suggestive buttressing of those claims that the beginning of humanity is located within her landmass, almost beyond dispute. A sense of mystery has always surrounded the land, and it brought numerous adventurers across her borders—and perhaps even a larger number transported thither only through imagination. Even for those who actually penetrated this vast tract of land, imagination was never loath to inject excitement into the terra incognita. European medievalists found in its accommodative belly a treasure trove for the bestiaries of their moralistic landscape, embroidered illuminated manuscripts with terrors that supposedly roamed its interior. Thus, for Africa, only centuries of calumny as bequests of the outer world, degradation, and, ultimately, depopulation, the consequences of which are still very much with her progeny. Could it ever have been otherwise?

On the other hand, could it be that Africa yet awaits discovery? This time, however, in the profound, not the geographical, sense, which makes no sense at all as a claim on any inhabited space. A continent yet waiting to be truly discovered—that is, virtually excavated, all magic and reality, myth and history, warts and beauty marks, as a proposition of universal challenge to facile preconceptions. And the first line of explorers should be—who else?—the indigenes themselves, astonished at what they had always taken for granted, or overlooked.

We shall begin from the external, then journey inward. A reluctance toward self-knowledge or, perhaps more precisely, toward reconciliation with self, may be overcome if one adopted a negative route:

begin by taking note of external assessments, damn them as products of ignorance, prejudice, and/or rank opportunism, then proceed to examine the possibility that, within today's matured offspring of "Mother Africa"—the nations—we also find authoritative voices which, with their own variations, appear to share the prejudices of the "fictionists" of her reality, the heirs of Herodotus. Where this is acknowledged we may then encounter grains of truth, or reasons for pause, for reconsideration, in confronting some of the jaundiced narratives about oneself. It is important to begin here, since the "discovery" that we urge must be primarily that of self, Africa being obviously in existence first and foremost for Africans before all others.

The possibility of uncovering externally inserted aspects of truth about one's reality may prove, paradoxically, to be of only secondary interest to the living generation. What may come to predominate in the very quest for survival on a continent in travail is the question of whether or not there will be found among a continent's own indigenes those who manifest the characteristics of external observers in their own clearly xenophobic enterprise. That Shakespeare's fictional creation, Othello, swears to the anatomical position of the human head among

> . . . the Cannibals that each other eat,
> The Anthropophagi, and men whose heads
> Do grow beneath their shoulders

is ultimately of only minor interest to the inhabitants of a continent whose own leadership often act as if their own people do not possess one shared head among them. This merely cautions us that there is always a choice for the partakers—voluntary or involuntary—in any form of relationship.

Let us imagine that a group of astronauts one day encounters some form of life in outer space—there are, after all, already hints of that possibility, even through analysis of uncovered meteorites on earth, and who knows what successors to the robot Sojourner may yet turn up on Mars! We shall therefore proceed to speculate that some form of sentient life, on whatever level of cultural or social development, is encountered on the surface of Mars. One such creature agrees to, or is seduced into, coming back to Earth with our adventurers, so that even we, the stay-at-homes, cannot pretend that the encounter was a televised hoax. Clearly the centrality, or the totality, of sentient existence lodged within our concept of humanity is dislodged forever. It is not simply a question of the comparative knowledge of oneself in relation to others; it is far more crucially the intrusive permanence of a potential extension of one's former scope of human perception and grasp of selfhood. The way we view and understand ourselves changes from then on, as does our view of the very universe that we have inhabited until then—very simply, it is no longer the same universe as before. It must qualify in some degree our social, productive, and even aesthetic perceptions, our spiritual assumptions, and our philosophical outlook. Africa continues to be a reservoir of such encounters, questioning preassumptions, both in major and minor keys—but of course only for the willing. This goes beyond the fact that, again and again, archeological digs on the continent continue to overturn, or at least question, confident attributions of human origin with a frequency that remains unmatched by any other continent. Of greater significance are the other exhumations, such as that of the kingdom of Kush, that narrate the hidden history of the socialized Homo sapiens, discoveries which assail given theories of—most pertinently—civilization, theories that have contributed to the convenient underrating, even dismissal, of that continent's contribution to such a universal pool.

The predominant pattern, alas, has been the temptation to take the easy way out, especially if there are motives that interpose themselves between us and a direct, truthful apprehension of the novelty. For instance, let us say that the aliens we have just encountered on that distant planet possessed mineral resources that we badly covet for our internal development, maybe even for further space exploration. Or perhaps the new discovered environment is so congenial to humans that we immediately think of expropriating it for settling our excess or idle population, converting it into an offshore plantation or tourist retreat. We then proceed to "evaporate" the new terrain as an inhabited space, its occupants rendered invisible. We prove to our satisfaction that these "aliens" are incapable of managing their own resources. We proceed to dismiss their history, downgrade their culture, pronounce them nonexistent or simply barbaric. Sustained by this opportunistic relegation, we take upon ourselves the holy mission of "civilizing" the newly encountered species, restoring it to human reckoning—albeit of a lower grade. Later generations are programmed, though a purposed filtering and dissemination of information, to cultivate a superior, condescending, or blatantly xenophobic agenda which graduates, over time, from mere denigrating observations, the dismissive wave of the hand, to a rigid theology. The literature of the early explorers of alien lands—Africa, the Americas, Asia, and Australasia—has played a crucial role in this self-arrogating proceeding.

That knowledge of Africa—including by Africans themselves— remains largely inchoate is thus a consideration that we cannot escape, given the nature of Africa's experience at the hands of the outside world, which has been largely one of violent repression and imposition. The "age of innocence" in encounters, before the conferment of one side with the status of the "protected," the converted, or the outright colo- nized, is a study in the collective psychology of the xenophobic which, it must be admitted, is not entirely restricted to the intruding human- ity. The attitude of the intruded upon can mostly be guaranteed to be either hostile curiosity or fear, or both. Exceptional are those instances where the intruder survives a response of fear in his hosts—that is, is not killed off outright but becomes a temporary guest (indulged adven- turer or trader) or graduates into a settler. Both sides then enter into mutual knowledge of each other as intriguing—but not fully understood— phenomenon. Many missionaries profited by this scenario, sometimes settling on land donated at a harmless distance from the rest of the host community, which proceeds to study them as a quaint organism under laboratory conditions. Such quaint organisms, alas, often evinced a re- markable penetrating capability, eventually overrunning and subjugating their hosts—having ensured reinforcements from more of their kind— lending credence to that ancient adage that warns "curiosity killed the cat."

Colonial experience demonstrated equally that the acquisition of knowledge between intruder and host occurs in fits and starts, with a reluctant gradualism and in a fragmentary fashion, where volunteered information may even contradict one's observations. This is simply part of the strategy of dominance—on the part of the intruder—of withholding truthful knowledge of himself and his kind. Mystery is allied to power, and a mystique is often deliberately inculcated in the mind of the host community in order to establish a relationship of awe and uncertainty. Where the agenda of the visitors is allied to exploitation of resources, these outsiders must present themselves as representatives of a superior civilization. It becomes expedient to suggest, as a policy of domination, that the receiving community is incapable of grasping the full immensity of history, achievements, and intelligence of the intruder. Two elements only are transmitted in their full panoply: one, its military power, and two, its religion. The rest is shrouded in mystery, and that includes knowledge of fellow aliens in other parts of the world.

The host entity, albeit from a different motivation, evinces a parallel attitude. Thus secrecy, or secretiveness, often emerges as the sole reliable commodity of exchange between stranger and host society. In the latter, however, let us note that it is simply a part of a self-defense mechanism—defense against real or suspected bad intentions of the visitor. A German intrusion—short-lived—experienced this in the nineteenth century at the hands of the Mende in West Africa, where a written version of the Vai language was kept secret so the Mende might communicate among themselves to the exclusion of their dangerous guests. Many researchers have screamed aloud, torn out their hair in frustration at the "clamminess" of some indigenous peoples whose cultures they have sought to penetrate in depth. There is invariably a certain level of deception on both sides. Suspicion is a healthy response to any new phenomenon.

Who is this creature that appears at once so similar and yet so different? That similarity poses the danger: he may want exactly what we have, and that craving may imperil our existence by reducing what we depend upon for survival. In short, both sides skirt the peripheries of truth, but while one is calculating, the other acts on instinct, self-protective and cautious. Both have a long tradition, beginning undoubtedly with the earliest unrecorded encounter among peoples, an event that we can only conjecture. We are wise to expect and to make allowances for it.

This intruder—armed with his flag—has to present himself as the representational totality of his kind outside the boundaries of the present. In any case such aliens are often in violent competition with one another on that same terrain, or in other parts of the globe. Thus it would be the exceptional German explorer who, of his own volition, imparted to his African audience any knowledge of the French or British as partakers in the same presumed attributes of a superior culture and level of development. Similarly, the British, French, etc., had to be the exclusive totality of civilization that is transmitted to the captive audience of the society on which they have imposed their presence. Thus was laid the foundation of surrogate rivalries among the colonized, with competing airs of superiority—francophone versus anglophone, lusophone against italophone, each and every one versus the rest in attitudes of condescension, mutual exclusion, and even outright belligerences, including surrogate wars that were diligently fueled by past masters of "divide and rule."

But first, let us give the devil his due. After all, the world's most famous epics have their roots in the history of intrusions. Human restlessness even aspires to be a very motor of productivity and development—

for one side or the other unquestionably—and has provided the world some of its most enduring literature and established archetypes in the literary pursuit for the delectation and, sometimes, enlightenment of humanity. For reasons that must be held to be flattering to the human mind, the adventure in itself, with its guaranteed baggage of novelty, appears to be never self-sufficient, but must be tied to some other "ennobling" design—as opposed to practical ones, such as opening up trade routes and embassies (including religious outposts). We have identified one such immaterial accretion and named it already—knowledge—the expansion of the existing boundaries of apprehension, one that transcends the mere cataloguing of external phenomena and attempts to delve into the nature of others, emerging (hopefully) with enhanced knowledge of one's self and place in an enlarged and more complex universe—the birth of anthropology. It dates from the earliest transmitted adventures that have come down in oral narratives and literature. Thus, to ensure that this point is not lost in the thrill of adventure, not drowned out in the clamor of swords on shields, in the torrent of blood and gore and at the boards of carousing, Homer imparts this lofty attribute to the archetypal adventurer, right at the beginning of his exordium in *The Odyssey:*

> He saw the townlands
> and learned the minds of many distant men.

Higher praise would be even more applicable to Ibn Batouta for his voyages through Africa, Asia, and the Far East. He was a far more meticulous historian than Herodotus and an even more adventurous voyager on land than Ulysses at sea. However, thanks to Homer, Ulysses offers himself more readily as the heroic exemplar, canonized in epic literature. Fortunately, he was more than simply a "renowned mariner" and adventurer but a student and chronicler of new experiences, in addition to being a shrewd psychologist; unfortunately, he also set a pattern for others—just as he was "formidable for guile in peace and war," a "sly and guileful man," he was also an acknowledged "master of improvisation"— in short, not averse to telling the proverbial fisherman's tall tale. Indeed, as Shakespeare also made a point of emphasizing in his delineation of the complex character of Ulysses, he was a man given to the arts of narrative embellishment, a compulsive raconteur of the exotic and often improbable. The nymph Calypso concedes that he is "not for nothing learned," and the mighty Zeus himself gave judgment that "there is no mortal half so wise." Let Ulysses plead the positive in the varied adventurers' escapades on the continent of Africa—Herodotus, Frobenius, Livingstone, Mungo Park, Joseph Thomson, André Gide, and all.

Unlike many of the "mere mortals," or, in some notable cases, even lesser than "mere mortals" of European colonial adventurism, Ulysses appears to have been, at least, a man of enviable intellectual and creative resources. One may claim that basically he was even anticolonialist or, more accurately, noncolonialist in orientation. We certainly do not read of him planting any Athenian flag on newly encountered lands, no matter how "primitive" their natives appeared to be. Ulysses had no "civilizing" agenda—all he desired was to go back home to his Penelope, who had kept her chastity belt in place, while Ulysses made souvenirs and trophies of numerous others en route.

One wonders, however, what the natives would have felt if they could eavesdrop on the accounts that Ulysses gave of the ways and customs of the many peoples it was his lot to encounter, the many distant men whose minds he ostensibly took pains to study. In all likelihood they would have had second thoughts about his powers of observation or judgment. The shock of such narratives would undoubtedly have modified the initial marvel at his very appearance among them, the skills of navigation that brought him there in the first place, or indeed the strangeness of his ways while he sojourned among them. Many, I am certain, would hardly recognize themselves in the accounts he would give of their daily lives, any more than would the inhabitants of Othello's world, a world that did indeed testify to Othello's stature as warrior and adventurer but one that he so shamelessly embellished in order to impress and win the fair Desdemona.

In another context I have had cause to refer to the writer as the frustrated explorer, sublimating his terror of the unknown in verbal, magical conquests of frontiers beyond the immediately accessible. Norman Mailer's famous paean to the first American intruders in outer space remains one of the most lavish, bravura testaments to this essence of the explorer *manqué* in the average writer. We need not go into the phenomenon of writers who have ennobled the genre of science fiction, and whose creations dominate the world of the cinema, plucking futuristic archetypes—if one may indulge in a pertinent oxymoron—out of virtual space. From our commencing remarks, however, it should be clear that the obverse of the coin does accurately complete the picture—the explorer or adventurer in his turn as the frustrated writer—and with what vengeance!

A single trajectory thus links Homer or Conrad with Herodotus, Hakluyt, Rider Haggard, Gide, or indeed Thomson, that knight-errant on a charger who remained persuaded of "a fair spirit of Africa," albeit obscured by villainous dragons in festering swamps. What separates literature from travelogue or chronicle is sometimes hazardous space for the consumer's navigational compass: in all cases the elements of inventiveness intrude, that trajectory of selectiveness, suppression, and distortion. They are never absent, any more than they are in the "letters home" of the latter-day tourist, intended only for the consumption of family and friends. Why should Africa expect to have been different?

The idyllic picture postcard, ready inscribed "Wish you were here" in order to conserve precious energy in the enervating regimen of tourist retreats, is, however, a far distant call from the desperate plunges of the earliest European explorers into *their* unknown, and the uneven literature that has survived their incursions. Africa was breeding ground for many of the *literati manqué*, who, in any case, mostly wrote home, "Thank God you are anywhere but here." Their demarcation of mountains, valleys, plains, and rivers in cold contours, their frequently naïve literary efforts to cope with strange cultures, histories, and sociologies may not match Shakespeare's stay-at-home conjurations of alien vistas— from *Anthony and Cleopatra* to *Troilus and Cressida*—but they nevertheless contribute to the pool of source material for subsequent writers, especially of the Victorian Age (as in the case of Daniel Defoe's *Robinson Crusoe*), source material that the societies of such writers required to complete a reasonably congruent model of the world—congruent, that is, with their own predilections, which they then promoted as the logical or divinely appointed order of the peoples of the world.

And yet a constant in the attitude of several of these adventurers on the African continent appears also to have been a sense of mystery, often highly romanticized from the first encounters. Thus the first arrivals in the kingdom of Monomotapa, on seeing the ruins of Zimbabwe, concluded that they had indeed stumbled on the legendary land of Ophir, the biblical supply source of riches to King Solomon. Frobenius, to return to the Teuton, never forgave the ancient civilization of Ile-Ife—in my own Yoruba part of Nigeria—for not being the lost city of Atlantis. The expression of his apoplexy is worth quoting at some length, since its vengeful, scabrous dismissal of the culture of an entire race, the Yoruba, captures, for many of his companion adventurers, the intensity of hostility toward an environment that they never could penetrate to any profound depths. Without even a smattering of the language of a people, Frobenius, like most of his colleagues, actually presumed himself capable of entering their thought processes, assessing their spiritual beliefs, or even partaking in the banquet of their daily discourse:

> There is an element of typical rigidity in the Ilifian [Frobenius' name for the native of Ile-Ife] and his intellectual poverty struck me repeatedly as being his most distinguishing quality. This, naturally, appears uncommonly strange to the historian of culture, and may at first seem surprising and unintelligible, on remembering that Ile-Ife is the religious centre, or as its people call it, the "navel" of the Yoruba socio-religious realm. This may sound contradictory, for the priesthood of a nation may, indeed, be reactionary, but it is very seldom deficient in thought.

The kernel of the conundrum offered by this singular African city is this, namely, that these people are managing an hereditary estate, whose creation is spiritually quite out of touch with their present conception of life. The people of Ile-ife lie like a slumbering dragon over the gold of a prehistoric treasure-house. Poverty-stricken in mind, because of their ignorance, they guard the old city which lends them respect, lofty position and religious supremacy because they reside in it, because the blood of its original founders and builders has been dissipated and evaporated by diffusion, but, most indubitably, not because the salvage has come down to the present in the external form of its original antique creation in an era of productive intellectual activity.

This was the fodder on which, in the main, the European mind of the late eighteenth, nineteenth, and early twentieth centuries were fed, a conditioning that has extended to much of its progeny till today, being reinforced by succeeding literature from the pens of writers like Joyce Cary, Aldous Huxley, but most notoriously Joseph Conrad. They made far more exciting reading than the clinical narratives, and were preferred, since they fulfilled a need for superior self-assessment, and justification for dreams of exploitation, including expansionist rivalries among European monarchs, their ministers, and businessmen.

There were contrasts, nonetheless, reliefs in contrast, where the mystery continent even basked in paradisal glow, but these were no match for the prosaic, even illustrated renditions that catered to the heroic image and the promise of profit to boot. In evocation of a distant idyll, none other than Lord Alfred Tennyson refused to be left out, even as a stay-at-home, though straining at the leash. Timbuktu was the shimmering oasis of many hearts' desire, but Tennyson at least tempered his vision with some caution. In 1829, as a student in Trinity College Cambridge, he won the Chancellor's prize for poetry with the poem *Timbuctoo:*

> "Wide Afric, doth thy sun
> Lighten, thy hills unfold a city as fair
> As those which starred the night o' the elder world?
> Or is the rumour of thy Timbuctoo
> A dream as frail as those of ancient time?"

> . . . . the time is well nigh come
> When I must render up this glorious home
> To keen Discovery; soon yon brilliant towers
> Shall darken with the waving of her wand;
> Darken, and shrink and shiver into huts,
> Black specks amid a waste of dreary sand
> Low-built, mud-walled, settlements.

A hundred years later, succeeding generations of the black exiles from the African homeland were still struggling to capture the essence of this continent of origination, struggling to rid themselves of the distortions inherited from their erstwhile owners and reestablish—at least in imagi-nation—the candidacy of remembered legends, but more as deliberate constructs, protest manifestoes to counter a negative reality as presented

by a racist society. Nor did some miss out on the chance of extending
this to an interrogation of the religious iconography of the very race
that had enslaved them. In *Heritage,* Countee Cullen's voice captured the
tenor of much of this dual service that was placed on the shoulders of
the Muse:

> What is Africa to me:
> Copper sun or scarlet sea,
> Jungle star or jungle track,
> Strong bronzed men, or regal black
> Women from whose loins I sprang
> When the birds of Eden sang?
> One three centuries removed . . .
>
> Lord, I fashion dark gods, too,
> Daring even to give You
> Dark despairing features where,
> Crowned with dark rebellious hair . . .

Freed of such impositions of race, social status, and history, and the demand of protest, the "Victorians" were free to give full rein to their parallel fantasies. Tennyson's friend, A. H. Hallam, was unrestrained in his
enthusiasm. Timbuctoo, standing for Africa, was the very stuff of idyll:

> Thou fairy City, which the desert mound
> Encompasseth, thou alien from the mass

Of human guilt, I would not wish thee found
Perchance thou art too pure . . .
Thy Palaces and pleasure-domes to me
Are matters of strange thought: for sure thou art
A splendour in the wild: and age to thee
Did visible guardians of the Earth's great heart
Bring their choice tributes, willed from many a mine,
Diamond, and jasper, porphyry, and the art
Of figured chrysolite: nor silver shine
There wanted, nor the mightier power of gold:
So wert thou reared of yore, City Divine!
And who are they of blisses manifold,
That dwell in thee.

More prosaically, but factually, a French scholar provides us in 1922 the base material from which the two Victorian poetasters could easily have drawn inspiration. Delafosse writes of a West African pre-Islamic State of 1353, "a real state, whose organization and civilization could compare favourably with that of Moslem kingdoms and of the same period." However, the trade in human flesh, and the need for its rationalization, had begun to take its toll, embarked on the task of eroding, first the fantasized and romaticized, then the factual, leading George Hardy to declare in 1927: "Islam began the work of destruction . . . but Europe did a better job." Africa was already open season. The writer, and indeed the graphic artist—for we must never forget that there still exist purported graphic representations of the marvels of these hitherto unexplored lands, several of whose originals have yet to be encountered till today—the artist, poet, or chronicler in the traveler continued the tradition of contracting or readjusting the frontiers of the real, and not, alas, always for the purpose of concision or artistic selectiveness—that is, abandoning the ordinary for the extraordinary, or for engaging, without unnecessary distraction, the humanistic sensibilities, impulses, and concerns of his readers. Jonathan Swift's caustic warning did little to deter them:

> Geographers, on Afric maps
> With savage drawings fill the gaps;
> And o'er uninhabitable downs
> Draw elephants for want of towns.

Was it much different in the time of Homer? Or, if we must maintain the distinction that he never pretended to be other than a spinner of imaginary epics—what of his countryman, the pioneer historian Herodotus? Herodotus was not above taking liberties with facts. He blithely improvised, in order to people, as it took his fancy, the "uninhabitable downs," those dark interiors of the African continent that he never actually penetrated. Homer's Ulysses, like Herodotus, may have "learned the minds of distant men" along the way, but if our archetypal adventurer had no qualms in spinning a yarn to deprive his own long faithful shepherd, a frail old man, of his cloak, in order to earn himself a warm night's sleep, who can blame Jonathan Swift's countrymen for also embellishing the truth on occasion in order to assure themselves sponsorship for future explorations, attract investors in the potential of future colonies, not to mention the prospects of future travels in greater personal comfort. Along the way, they would lay the foundations for an empire, racing against time and against other competitors from Germany, Spain, Italy, France, Holland, and Portugal.

This multidimensional excursion into the past "fictioning" of Africa is of course a salutary reminder of a tendency that we, on our part, had always considered part of the long tradition of Eurocentrism, with all its negative and only occasionally positive implications. The concerted fictioning of Africa by imperial powers, known by its more familiar name—partitioning—is simply a continuation of the superimposition of speculation, interest, or willed reality over history and fact by direct means, and it requires its own separate and more tragic treatment. Africa remains the monumental fiction of European creativity. Every so-called nation on that continent is a mere fiction perpetrated in the cause of external interests by imperial powers, a fiction that both colonial rule and post-independence exertions have struggled and failed—in the main—to turn into an enduring, cohering reality. It is a gross fiction whose exposure continues to exact penalties in hundreds of thousands of lives—Rwanda-Burundi, Mauritania, Liberia, Somalia, and, most lately, Sudan, etc.—one that only a few governments, such as Ethiopia, have had the courage to stand on its head and creatively interrogate. The Ethiopian example, albeit under compulsion, resulted in the mutual dissolution of that piece of real estate, and its reemergence in two nation entities. For others the will remains lacking. To have swept Tiv from Nigeria's Northern Plateau and Ijaw from the Delta region together into a shotgun marriage, or Luo and Gikuyu willy-nilly into an inchoate modern state, was as egregious a fiction as Othello's armpit-cradled African head. Workable or not, the external arbitrariness of such an act, undertaken without even a cynical expression of consideration for the histories, cultures, and economic usages of their peoples, but as mere conveniences of the external will, was doomed to have dire repercussions. Africa has paid, and continues to pay, a heavy price for the upkeep of a European fiction.

The fictioning of African humanity is an integral part of the same enterprise of landscape apportionment as illustrated in the sample experiences to which we have already referred. The preponderant tenor of the downgrading of that humanity has naturally drawn contestations in the past century as nation after nation of the continent found its voice, and as protagonists even more learned than Ulysses or Frobenius, and more methodical, rose to redress the narratives. These voices are now heard in the works of notable historians, philosophers, and ethnologists such as Theophilus Ki Zerbo of Burkina Faso, Adu Boahen of Ghana, Kenneth Dike and Jacob Ajayi of Nigeria, Mudimbe of the Congo, Paulin Houtoundji of Benin, Cheikh Anta Diop of Senegal, to cite predominantly from the West Coast of Africa, the coast that has provided the most enduring and resilient African cultures and spirituality in the Americas, followed by the Congo. Not surprisingly, this also constitutes that portion of the African continent that has held such inspirational attraction for the great Diaspora pan-Africanists—George Padmore, W. E. B. Du Bois, Edward Blyden, Sylvester Williams, Jean Price-Mars, among others. It was that African subregion that Du Bois chose as his final home and eventual resting place. The remedial enterprise has been pursued in fiction and poetry through the works of Sheik Hamidou Kane of Senegal, Mazizi Kunene of South Africa, Ahmadou Koroumba of Mali; then Maryse Conde, Daniel Maximin and Aimé Césaire, Derek Walcott, and others, all of especial interest since they not only deal with the African experience of empire and slavery from their own far-flung borders, they involve in their literatures the reconstructed histories of the West African peoples. Antonio Olinto and Zora Zeljan, Brazilians of European descent, Nicolás Guillén of Cuba, Abdias do Nascimento, the Rottweiler of African cultural assertion in Brazil, have also contributed to this factional reconstruction of Africa's humanity, in works of prose and religious drama, while the American Chancellor Williams foraged deeply into African antiquity in his lifelong mission to undo the petulant attribution of Africa's civilization to non-African sources. As for the Englishman Basil Davidson, his numerous works assiduously linked both past and present, seeking, it sometimes appears, an explanation for that present in the ruins of the past.

We have invoked a roll call of these scholars and fiction writers—both of the continent and the Diaspora—in order to propose them as material of critique for our latter-day internal descendants of the fictioning tradition, glancingly mentioned earlier on, who, very often, are to be found at the pinnacle of political power or among their courtiers and apologists. This class presents us with a rather bemusing, even ironic tendency, because, even while they proclaim their fundamental agenda to be one of recovery of racial dignity—*authenticité, africanité,* the African Personality, etc., etc.—that is, claim reconstructive authority over

the history of racial self and its destiny, their actual conduct consolidates
the promotion and validation of the earlier fictioning of a continent by
external voices and interests.

This has proved one of the root causes of what is often referred to
as the crisis of African emergence into modernity, and it is largely a crisis
of leadership alienation.

To fully appreciate the enormity of this enterprise we need only
attempt to grasp the emergence of individuals or classes from within the
suppressed, the negatively regarded partners in the narrated encounters,
objects of condescension at best, who now proceed to inaugurate a new
era and axis of differentiation with the same mentality of domination
and/or exploitation—in short, carry on the agenda of the original intruders. It is useful to bear constantly in mind the context from within
which this neo-fictioning takes root.

It constitutes a profound indictment, for it has to do with both
the contradiction between the history and reality of the African continent on the one hand, and the contrived perception of the rulers on
the other—which is why we must call attention to the work of both
scholars and other professionals in authenticated history, in addition to
outright fiction that establishes its own modalities of authentification
from within the actualities of peoples and their experience, manners,
and relationships. Armed with such works, one can only wonder on
what diet the neo-fictionists of African historic reality have been fed.
It is clear that their choice of direction in this project of revisionism
reveals—in comparison with their foreign predecessors—a far more

alienated mentality and exocentric agenda, for which Africa's humanity continues to pay a heavy price. Thomson at least permitted himself
acknowledgment of the existence of "the fair spirit of Africa," in pursuit of which he was prepared to undergo the privations and perils of
the unknown. Not so his latter-day indigenous successors. For these
their fellow Africans have not evinced any quality that qualifies them
as possible habitations of that "fair spirit." They offer them coercion in
the manner of Stanley and Livingstone, at best paternalism, a political
broth on which Africans have retched for centuries even as it was forced
down their throats by recognizable aliens. What is sad, for many, is that
such secessionists—for this is what they are, secessionists from the common African experience—appear to remain blissfully ignorant of their
antecedents; they simply are unaware of the racist cause that their pronouncements and actions champion.

How recently was it, for instance, that the colonizing powers
strained every muscle to delay the independence of their colonial holdings on the pretext that their subjects were simply "not ready for self-
governance"? Or perhaps we should travel even further back, to the
philosopher schools of Hegel, Gobineau, David Hume, etc. What they
presented as studied results of the racial encounter was simply that the
black races had no skills of governance, no arts, no sciences, that their
only salvation lay in being ruled by superior minds—the Caucasians,
naturally. Albert Schweitzer refined this scholarly finding by conceding
that the African was admittedly his sibling, but very definitely a junior
one in need of the disciplining relationship of an adult to a child, but

Cardinal Verdier, Archbishop of France, spells out the ideal relation in even more unctuous form, a far cry from Delafosse:

> Nothing is more moving than this gesture of the French-
> man, taking his black brother by the hand and helping him
> to rise. This hierarchic but nonetheless black collaboration,
> this fraternal love stooping toward the blacks to measure
> their possibilities of thinking and feeling . . . this art, in a
> word, of helping them progress through wise development
> of their personality toward an improved physical, social and
> moral well-being; this is how France's colonizing mission on
> the black continent appears to us.

How do these differ from the claims of Africa's latter-day one-party rulers or outright dictators who blithely announce to the world that the African is so singularly politically underendowed that he cannot be permitted to participate in the processes of governance or contribute his or her voice to the choice of his leaders? It would appear, however, that God, in his infinite contradiction, has placed among such retarded peoples the exceptional individuals, strategically positioned at the departure of the colonial rulers, to take over power and hang on to it for eternity. Either that, or ensured that within each nation's military there would always be found a budding dictator, divinely primed for assuming the white man's burden of ruling the black race—preferably with an iron rod, and heated, in emulation of the former slave owners' branding proclivity. Sometimes the divine wand is seen to have descended not on one individual head but on a group, thus implicitly, or even overtly, in unambiguous pronouncements, excluding all others from the role of governance.

For a long time after independence, Kenya was indeed one such simmering pot of discontent that would finally boil over in 2009. From the Nigerian political class, the nation was once openly instructed on the divine appropriateness of such a hegemonic theology by an apologist of feudal control. He provided a particularist variant that may yet prove to be the rock upon which the fiction that is the Nigerian nation eventually founders. Designating the three major ethnic constituencies of the nation by supposedly inherent attributes—and thus even excluding over three hundred others from leadership considerations—this politician, a former ambassador to the United Nations, declared, without the slightest concession to its potential for chaos: "God in his infinite wisdom has provided different peoples with different talents. The Igbo," he elaborated, "have been provided the gift of entrepreneurship. The Yoruba make first-class administrators and educationists. The North"— home of the Hausa/Fulani, his ethnic group—"is however singularly endowed with the gift of leadership." To attempt to challenge such a divine ordering would, of course, amount to an act of impiety. Substitute Belgium's declarations of its "civilizing" mission in the Congo, or the Germans' divinely justified credo in Namibia, and we find ourselves on all too familiar ground. How tragic for a continent that in the year 2010, a nation ruled by a historian, Laurent Gbagbo, heir to numerous schools of Enlightenment, was again brought teetering on the brink of violent disintegration by that same cast of mind, having drunk from the poisoned chalice of that exclusivity communion with the local name of *ivoirité!*

The thesis is no longer the alien master race versus the inferior but the master caste against the rest of society, the divinely appointed shepherd among a mindless flock. Difficult to starkly proclaim that history, culture, human talent, merit, or aptitude do not matter, the modern refiners of the doctrine of divine rule take refuge in merely implying that such distinctions do not matter in equal measure—thus putting paid to the contrary view that is summed up in a much abused yet tenacious concept: democracy. The first-comers in the stakes of power after colonialism have made this the consistent policy of governance: Actualize power, then fictionalize the people.

3.   Fictioning of the Fourth Dimension

Africa must come to terms with her past. Only this will enable
her to establish an honest and mutually respectful relationship
with the outside world enabling all parties in this dismal history
to inaugurate a new era of interaction. To this end, we must establish the total truth on slavery—both the TransSaharan and the
TransAtlantic; the partition of the continent; colonisation; even
the secretive dumping of toxic wastes on the African continent,
and call attention to the deleterious effects of these experiences
on Africa's present.

Millennium Commission report, 2001

ALL IN ALL, WE CAN IDENTIFY FOUR schools of fictioning—we have already encountered three—one is the purely driven adventurer's; the second the commercial (Stanley, King Leopold, Kaiser Wilhelm, etc.), and
the third the internal, power-driven fictioning by their successors. There
is a fourth, one that surfaces from time to time and appears destined

to remain the theme that often dominates cross-continental exchanges between Africa and her Diaspora.

To this last, it is possible to concede positive motivations—such as the desire to redress history and generate a momentum for restitution from historic despoilations, in whatever form. However, the extreme and dogmatic of this school often slide down the chute of emotionalism and drop into the same ancient pit of self-gratification, ultimately self-undermining. The issue is not really whether or not the claims for—yes, here comes the word!—Reparations are tenable or not, the danger is that in pursuit of this agenda, an Africa that never did exist is created, history is distorted, and even memory abused. An argument for Reparations between aggressor and victim can still survive evidence that the victim side was not completely innocent in its own undoing—be it through negligence or direct complicity. A charge of burglary is not vitiated by clear evidence of an "inside job"—which might include having left a window open for the intruders. Where the house owner stubbornly denies clear evidence of internal dereliction, however, he effectively becomes an accessory to future robbery and loses the moral right to restitution, or, indeed—justice!

Nothing of this minimizes or extenuates the enormity of the crime against a continent or excuses an attempt to gloss over it through contrasts or exercises in relativity. Yet comparisons are not valueless in themselves, since they can serve as a process of clarifying the claims of subjectivity. There are certain voyage stops—like the bookmark—inserted into any attempt to review the world's accounting of a receding millennium, stops that are likely to remain pertinent to succeeding generations, and for centuries. Most individuals have their sobering lists, a mere recollection of which checks them in stride even in the midst of marveling at or celebrating the undeniable, often unthinkable leaps in human achievements. It would be astonishing if the average list does not contain one or both of the following: the Holocaust and Hiroshima. For most Africans at home or dispersed, however, there is a third.

The first two may eventually congeal into cautionary metaphors of a vanishing past—that is, the events that gave them life occurred as a one-in-an-era event, an aberration, albeit of tremendous, world-altering impact. The effects are not over, nor will they have evaporated any time soon, especially the first—the Holocaust. The third—already given name a number of times—is a far more elusive, insidious, and seemingly eternal condition. It is also, paradoxically, a self-attenuating metaphor, which perhaps accounts for its tenacity, since it encourages a tendency toward toleration. In other words, on the one hand, one would not dare say, "Oh, some forms of the Holocaust, or Hiroshima, are more benign than others." These terms tersely provoke outright rejection—Never Again!— except of course for a psychopathic minority.

The third offers evidence not even of the short memory of the world but of the regard with which the African continent is held, since it is one that would leap instantly to head such a list for the average African. By contrast, it would have to be near forcefully impressed on others as a candidate for such a list. I have encountered this cast of mind—that is, requiring reeducation, at several gatherings dedicated to Memory, Race Relations, Human Rights, Conflict Resolution, Reconciliation strategies— and allied themes. It is indeed revealing of much else, since this third bookmark happens to lack the consolation of being in a terminal past—unlike the Holocaust or Hiroshima, it lacks an identifiably limited duration. The most commonly encountered proof of that claim, its predictable absence from a global list of human negativities, is lodged in the frequently encountered lament that the earliest question mark on the much-acclaimed European humanism was the Holocaust. I have long and fervently contested this, and each time obtained a restrained, grudging retraction, almost condescending, mostly lacking in conviction.

This benchmark, bookmark, watershed—it is all of these and much more—was itself the logical product of a much older, enduring phenomenon, one of those aspects of human relationship that often does not "quite know itself." People do not quite know what to make of it, whether or not to even acknowledge its existence in the present. Certainly anachronistic, its most quantitative, structured manifestation qualifies it to be deemed, like the other two, a universal memory blot that might even be entered in the ledger books as yet another once-in-an-era occurrence, but what a prolonged era, spanning centuries! Yes, indeed, we have in mind the African slave trade. The phenomenon begets the event, but even when the event is over, or is at least formally declared ended, residual forms—which antedate the structured manifestation, the slave trade itself—also survive and perpetuate the basic phenomenon, which is slavery, enslavement, servitude. This is when the earth of perpetuation of a grievous crime has cause to examine itself carefully, see whether or not the finger pointed at exterior violators also curves inward to implicate the descendants of the victims of a crime of global dimensions, one that yet remains immersed in the phenomenon itself—slavery. Slavery in seductive dressing, slavery as the foundation of contradictory internal relationships, slavery by that or any other name, a phenomenon that constantly reinvents itself.

Let us settle the crime of "they" right away as being beyond dispute. It is established, amply documented in every conceivable medium—memoirs, gravures, watercolors, extant markets, decrees, legislations, theses, performance, plastic arts, demographic maps, the cinema, commemorations, etc., etc. This crime is branded into collective memory. The forts alone, strategically placed, dotting not only the coastline but massively testimonial also in parts of the interior, settle the guilt of "they" beyond question. That leaves "us," and the necessity of a truthful internal reckoning.

We should therefore embark without further distraction on a journey to that place that was actually designated at one time, and indeed enshrined in some atlases, as the Slave Coast—with the same system of commodity labeling as the Gold Coast, Ivory Coast, Oil Coast, etc. Our first stop is the slave depot of Badagry, on the southwest coast of Nigeria. Badagry is a good place to begin our journey since it has been in the news in recent years—on the BBC and al Jazeera, at least—and with some controversy, having been designated the location for a large-scale holiday resort development with a theme park. That park will contain casinos, golf courses, cinemas, shopping malls, museums, etc. The controversy was over whether or not this is an appropriate setting for the tourist industry, as it is a place of tears and bitter memory. The pro argument is that African-Americans, instead of spending their vacation dollars in European watering holes—Paris, Rome, Cannes, Venice—should be encouraged to make a pilgrimage to a place of memory and instruction, but also, in the process, fun and leisure. It is, after all, meant to be a vacation resort. The critics claim that this is using one hand to wipe the foam of tears from the eye and the other the foam from a tankard of beer.

There is, however, more to the slave trade than tears. The African slavery experience has also recorded moments of resilience and triumph, and these are worthy of retention in memory and of commemoration. Taste and judgment may prove the ultimate test. The chosen theme for the theme park is, incidentally, the Jackson Five, with Michael Jackson as the reigning icon—paintings, sculptures, photos, round-the-clock screening of videos and films, all the usual memorabilia. We shall leave the pros and cons, the appropriateness or banality of the entire project to another place. The question that really matters for some of us is: Will visitors be offered a complete, uncensored presentation of history? Or will that ugly, escapist import from other parts of the world—Political Correctness—govern the offerings that the returnees encounter? Shall we appropriate the coy scissors of censorship? For the moment, let us ask why the choice of this place anyway. What actualities does it record? Well then, here is the tale of two families in that very town of Badagry, descendants of some notable participants in history who are still very much alive and not only thriving but also rivals.

The first is the Mobee family. Its history of prominence and affluence goes back to the nineteenth century, principally as a result of the lucrative participation of its head, Chief Mobee, in the slave trade.

According to records, Chief Mobee was one of the eight Badagry chiefs who eventually signed the treaty of abolition of the trade in the Badagry district—in addition to conceding the district to the British as the property of their king forever. This pattern of piecemeal colonization is common knowledge, the project of scattered acquisitions that would later be consolidated by the Berlin Treaty of the Partition of Africa in 1881. In order to give legitimacy to the claims of such nations as Germany, Italy, Great Britain, and France, these nations either bought over chiefs and got them to put their thumbprint to paper, or they overran them by superior force of arms, planted their flags, and presented the fact of occupation to Berlin for recognition by their fellow adventurers. Chief Mobee was not only a slaving tycoon, he ceded portions of the West African land and patrimony to British powers.

Our second family is that of Seriki Williams Faremi Abass. Now Mr. Faremi Abass was a pointer in the direction of our theme—one of many of this kind. I have elsewhere acknowledged a constant astonishment at the capacity of those who had endured the condition of enslavement to ever consider enslaving their own kind. Abass was, in his own person, a direct embodiment of that transformation. He was a native of a once-famous town called Aiyetoro, again in the southwestern Yoruba part of present Nigeria, and was sold into slavery at the age of six. He succeeded in escaping and fled to Badagry. After eking out a living for a number of years—a bit of farming and commodity trading—he found his real calling, which was to become a middleman to the Brazilian slave merchants. At this point, however, the slave trade was already entering its unpopular phase through the efforts of the abolitionist crusade.

Chief Mobee appeared to have heeded the call, because he sold some of his slave baracoons—as the preshipment holding pens for slaves were called—to Seriki Abass. Wrong move. Bad business decision. Seriki expanded and became more prosperous and influential in the trade than Chief Mobee. Well, this was where it all began, a rivalry between families that has persisted till today, even into Nigerian contemporary politics.

Rivalries often prove productive. This particular rivalry led to each creating a family museum of its own for the preservation of some of the relics and documents of their activities in the flesh trade. The Seriki museum contains personal items, domestic and trade related, of the great slave trader—robes, porcelain plates and bowls—all symbols of class and affluence, gifts as well as trophies presented to Seriki Abass by his Brazilian partners. Original posters, advertising the arrival of new consignments, and sales invoices have been preserved, as well as a letter or two of appreciation from the Brazilians to their business partner. There are early Bakelite phonograph records. Photographs show the chief in a meeting with his foreign business associates. Needless to say, there are relics such as shackles, chains, and other restraining equipment for slaves to ensure that they remained secure in their baracoons until shipment time. Overlooking the entrance into the baracoon, which, for security, can be gained only from within the compound itself, is perhaps the most imposing feature of the courtyard: the ornate, well-preserved grave of Seriki Faremi Abass.

If you do visit Badagry you will be taken on a walk along the sands, now clearly marked, toward the spot of embarkation. Today, a modern monument marks this Point of No Return. Along the way you will have passed a huge sunken water pot, remarkably well preserved. It is known as the Well of Attenuation. Every slave was made to stop and drink from it, since the water was laced with some kind of potion—or perhaps simply psychic potency!—that supposedly induced a state of amnesia. Their past was completely wiped away, and the captives moved submissively into a new state of existence—slavehood.

We continue our tour. On to Ouidah, which has preserved its slaving memories even more meticulously, including a similar walk along the sands to the point of embarkation, but over a wooden plank walkway. Instead of the Well of Attenuation it boasts a Tree of Forgetfulness, around which the slaves were made to do a ritual dance for the same purpose—induction of amnesia. The coastal slaves were all destined, with very few exceptions, for the notorious transatlantic passage toward the Americas.

Now let us change our coastline trajectory and travel northward, passing through Ghana toward the Sahelian region. The inland equivalents of the slave baracoons, forts, and dungeons of the British, Dutch, French, and Portuguese on the coastal areas are the massive slave camps, relics of which exist till today. Slavery scholarship—just a footnote—tends to ignore the fact that the European slave merchants themselves occasionally ventured deep into the interior to buy from the slave camps, although of course it was mainly the African middlemen who bought the slaves, then marched them down to the coast to the baracoons and waiting ships. Not so detailed also is the fact that a number of these slaves went northward, marching with caravans through Timbuktu, Mauritania to Morocco, Algeria and Egypt, some ending

up in Syria and Lebanon and other Arab states. Black ghettoes—that
is, quarters occupied by African slave descendants—exist in northern
and northeastern Arab countries. It is Morocco, however, that actually
boasts a predominantly black city—as opposed to ghettoes—populated
by escaped slaves and the manumissioned. The name of that town is Es-
saoiura, on the coast, also increasingly becoming a tourist destination.

The holding conditions of the slaves in their camps find contemporary echoes. They serve as metaphors for the actualities of a few hundred millions of presumed free men, women, and children on the continent within their own nations, with no experience or memory of being
enslaved or displaced. Here are a few snapshots from these northern
camps.

The Pikworo Slave Camp is located in the Upper East Region of
Ghana, in the town of Paga, itself a strategically located town between
the borders of Ghana and Burkina Faso. Here flourished the ancient
Pikworo Market, a major transit camp for slaves. The marketing and
transportation process was no different from what we know of the coastal
trade. Slaves were sorted into different categories of marketability, and
the ones found fit enough would be selected for the onward journey
to the major slave market at Salaga in the Northern Region. Sickly or
otherwise unfit slaves—among whom must be counted the rebellious—
were simply disposed of and buried. Slaves were obviously cheaper in
the interior than on the coast, which explained why the European trad-
ers themselves occasionally risked the journey north. Even today the
large piece of land on which the camp was located, a rocky and desert

environment, bears the physical landmarks of the trade as it was crudely executed.

Eating arrangements, incredibly, provide us a glimpse into their degrading condition. To ensure that they were reduced, virtually, to the status of beasts, they were denied any semblance of plates and bowls. Instead, the captives were made to chisel hollows in the rock surface, using stones. Four to five slaves gathered round each scooped-out plate to eat the regulated amount, just sufficient to keep them alive, not enough to enable them become so strong as to attempt escape or rebellion. Albeit smoothed by time and weather, the eating holes gouged into those rocks symbolize the permanent scars of dehumanization still borne by the indigenes of that continent, and their condition as glorified slaves within their own nations.

Some other names to keep in mind: Salaga, Sandema, Nalerigu, Gwollu, Jenini, Samp, Kafaba, Kintampo—the last two being interior embarkation and disembarkation points across Lake Volta. Those destined for the transatlantic slave route were marched through Bolgatanga and Kumasi in the Ashanti region and down to the custom-built forts. Those marked for the trans-Sahara slave route—which took on an exponential increase as the abolitionist movement of the late eighteenth and nineteenth century squeezed the coastal slave traffic, leaving their owners with largely empty baracoons—were taken to Tamale, to Burkina Faso and Mali, and on to North Africa and other Arab states. They joined the caravan trail of the much older traffic, along which marched victims of the Arabo-Berber slave raids on Somalia, Ethiopia, the Sudan, and

Niger, and over which were transported supplies from collaborative commerce with the local chiefs such as we have already outlined on the west coast. Quite a number journeyed farther eastward—Saudi Arabia, Qatar, Dubai, and Iran—to be united with those voyagers from East Africa—Tanzania and Zanzibar. These had made their passage in dhows across the Indian Ocean. Among the sinister elisions in the story of the African dispersal is that of the far more ancient slave trade that commenced at least a millennium before the transatlantic and continued long after the abolitionist movement had staunched the latter.

A final image: There is no shortage of tumuli and other burial signs in these slaving areas where expired slaves are buried, some of them alive, but none of these matches the iconic presence of one lone baobab tree over a tract of land in Salaga, next to a river. No tumulus will be found on this spot. Among the branches of that baobab tree is tied a white cloth, now somewhat browned and weather-worn, on which we read the community's pledge against slavery. That baobab tree marks the disposal grounds of what I have termed "expired" slaves. In this particular market town of Salaga, the slaves were not buried, they were simply dumped on the land. Thus the river that flows by that tract of land became known as *Rafi angalu*—the river of vultures. The vultures perched or hovered obligingly, swooping down at their leisure to carry out their scavenging on the open graveyard.

The history of Africa is the narrative of the Great Dispersal—westward, eastward, and northward, those latter two vectors being much understated. In truth, the perpetrators of that crime against Africa's humanity

confront us with the chastening fact that history is not always simplisti-
cally a "versus" narrative—us against those or others. And even if it were,
history also demonstrates that, sooner or later, the chickens come home
to roost. An instructive expression for humanity but—wait a moment—
is this not one that has taken on a new meaning, indeed, a contrary
meaning to what that expression originally intended? A reversal has
taken place, no less than a historic spin. For where, in all our study of
history, did we expect that one chicken would come to roost in the tall-
est tree on the landscape of reversals, looking down, so to speak, on the
rest of humanity in their holding pens. The "coon" of yesteryear, a mere
trade commodity, descendant of inmates of the baracoons of contempt,
sits on a pinnacle of power, the wheel of the world in his hands to steer
to a destination of crash or safety. It was a moment to savor undoubtedly, but only briefly. It is a season of sobriety for the African continent,
a moment for the resumption of decades of interrupted but now clam-
orous stock-taking—but with a revolution in orientation.

The dance is over. Like the toes of a corpse in a shallow grave, the
hibernating buds of realities push their way to the fore. This is a time
when all thinking Africans and African-Americans must ask themselves
why, in Kenya, one of the most popular of the songs composed to salute
the ascent of Obama to power goes: "It is easier for a Luo to become
president of the United States than to be president of Uganda" (Luo is
a minority tribe in Uganda). That song is an indictment that goes to
the roots of Africa's woes, the bane of the mentality of exclusivity from
which racist encampments like the United States are finally emerging—
one, however, that continues, ironically, to plague a continent whose

history has been one of a collective exclusivity of its inhabitants from human designation, certainly in global reckoning.

Close on the heels of the eight-year headship of the United Nations by Kofi Annan, an indigene of that nation whose notoriety in the hunting and transportation of his ancestors is not denied by their descendants at home, some of whose ancestral victims are among the bleached bones that line the trans-Sahara slave route, comes another elevation to global authority of another indigene whose ancestors, or ancient kin, were transported in dhows across the Indian Ocean and perhaps participated in the revolt of the Zanj in Iraq or ended up in the black ghettoes of Aleppo or Damascus. If this does not make a Robert Mugabe think, the fundamentalist warlords of Somalia pause, the Omar Bashirs of the Sudan and the Congolese abusers of African humanity reflect, then Africa has ceased to matter, even in the concerns of her inhabitants. The history of any violent dispersal is the history of genocide, and genocide is the name of much of the scenario now being played out and reenacted over and over again right on the continent, perhaps most systematically in nations like the Sudan. The internal criminality of the past has translated into the impunity of the present. As long as that past is fictionalized or denied, Africa is doomed to the curse of repetition, albeit in disguised, even refined forms. Instances are numerous, but none so flagrant, none so attributable to the failure to transcend a past of inhuman race relations, as the conduct of an unrepentant ruling class of Sudan. There the sacred space of memory is indeed preserved—and abused—while the rest of the world reposes under the shade of the Tree of Forgetfulness.

4. The Tree of Forgetfulness: Alive and Well in Darfur

A DRAMATIST BY PROFESSION, I AM most partial to rituals. There is, however, one ritual I would rather the world had never known. It has already received mention, and it ranks in my mind as one of the bleakest, most mentally eviscerating rituals that I have ever encountered in decades of exploring the world of dramatic rituals. This ritual took place on the coast of the ancient city of Ouidah, in the present-day Republic of Benin, and its centerpiece was that tree named, for its very function, the Tree of Forgetfulness.

The function was this: when slaves were brought from the inland towns and settlements of West Africa, usually victims of wars and raids engendered for that very purpose, they were placed in stockades, forts, and castle dungeons—the West African coastline is dotted with these—then, before embarkation, subjected to ritual processes which included moving in circles around that infamous tree. The purpose was to make them forget their land, their homes, their kinfolk, and even the very occupations they once knew—in short, forget their former existence, wipe their minds clean of the past and be receptive to the stamp of strange places. Yet another explanation of this ritual leans toward a response to the fear in those vendors that their victims, if they happened to die in exile—as was extremely likely—might return to haunt their violators. Whichever was the predominant intent, one thing was certain: these flesh merchants of their own kind understood that their act constituted a profound transgression, and they moved to thwart anticipated reprisals through the ritual process.

Never was optimism more misplaced—as a ritual, it was a complete failure. Those slaves never forgot, and one's mind often attempts to lock onto the mechanisms of those long-vanished minds, minds that were of the victims' same earth, same history, same nurturing—the African slave hunters and middlemen. *They* thought up that ritual, not the alien invaders. One's habit of evocation takes the mind to those surreal moments of a shackled, circling humanity, wondering how many such trees exist, even symbolically, all over the landscape of other peoples, other races and nations.

That very Tree of Forgetfulness survives today in all its bloodied glory, and, next to it, there is a tell-tale mound. That mound is a tumulus, the resting place of those slaves who could not wait to reveal that the ritual of forgetfulness lacked potency. They rebelled, refused to step on the ships' gangways, attempted to escape or foment uprisings, and were slaughtered. But even those who embarked and were shipped across to another world did not forget, and that world, or parts of that world, anyway, have never been permitted, or permitted themselves to forget, at least not in contemporary times. This is why for most of the year 2007, several nations—the United Kingdom, the Caribbean, France and her colonies, and the Commonwealth member states especially—rallied to the commemoration of the two hundredth anniversary of the abolition of the slave trade in Great Britain and her former possessions.

Most Africans would prefer to forget the Tree of Forgetfulness, just as their descendants in the United States would also choose to forget—at least judging from the emotive reactions, rising to virulent denunciations from a number of African-American and African scholars and commentators, to a television series that did nothing more than state, factually, that the Tree of Forgetfulness has its roots on African soil, and that the processes—ritualistic or commercial—that desecrated so much of Africa's humanity implicated, ironically and embarrassingly, the very race that produced millions of such victims. Don't we all love to eat of the exonerating fruit of the Tree of Forgetfulness? We are not alone, however, though that is no consolation. It is the legacy of eating of that fruit, no matter by whom, that confronts us today. In other contexts I have proposed that it is that primordial sin, the eating of that "forbidden fruit," that accounts for the proliferation of new slave plantations on the African continent, presided over by succeeding generations of Simon Legrees in black skin, even into contemporary times. Former slaves, black and African, now lifted on economic tides, are documented as having themselves turned slave owners in the United States, the very nation where discourse on reparations rages the fiercest. Surprising to some? An unthinkable, fiercely contested notion to many, especially ultra-nationalist African-Americans? But why? Did those "turned" slaves, now capitalist flesh merchants, not merely continue an economic pattern that was prevalent in their originating homeland? No matter, the records are there, incontrovertible.

Perhaps they have forgotten, or they believe that history itself is

a shackled captive that should by now have made its final circle around
the Tree of Forgetfulness. Others have not, neither races nor national
or global institutions. And the reasons for this are multiple. For a start,
even the bleakest histories yield moments of elevation, and humanity is
further impoverished when it permits itself to jettison such passages of
courage, resilience, and survival, even transformation of the minds of
the violators, and their efforts at restitution. The world requires such
uplifting ironies. Thus, for a number of years, UNESCO has promoted
the ritual of the International Day for the Remembrance of the Slave
Trade and Its Abolition, celebrated annually. Understandably, that commemoration took on a special character in 2007, being a bicentennial.
My view, however, is that not even that year's notation could match the
historic gravity of another two hundredth anniversary, which occurred
three years earlier, in 2004.

Does that year ring a bell? Well, the year 2004 happens to have
enjoyed the additional recognition of the independence date of the Republic of Haiti, recent victim of one of the most disastrous earthquakes
that any people have endured throughout the past century. Perhaps that
crumb of heroic solace from the past will sustain the recovery process,
which, at first glance, struck one as a near-impossible task. Certainly it
provoked among some the whimsical consideration of a reverse journey
into the continent's bosom, from which they were so brutally extracted
over three centuries ago. The government of Senegal wasted no time in
taking the humanitarian plunge, bringing back to Senegal the first organized wave of black repatriates since the establishment of Liberia in 1822
for the resettlement of freed slaves. But this was—and rightly so—an

isolated relief gesture. Even in its prostrate condition, and despite its own contemporary history of villainous, demonic rulers, such as "Papa" and "Baby Doc" Duvalier, depressing echoes of the Mother Continent's own Idi Amins and Macias Nguemas, the liberation of Haiti for the black dispersal is such a heroic chapter for the continent and for the world that the island's physical stature as a mere dot in the Caribbean Sea, constantly at the mercy of hurricanes—and now, earthquakes—has been transformed into a promontory for the comprehensive seizure of the essence of freedom.

Haiti remains the first black republic of the modern world, founded and governed by descendants of slaves and thus the symbol of revolt against human enslavement throughout the New World, and a beacon for the spirit of freedom anywhere. This includes Iraq, where a rebellion of African slaves—known as the Zanj—held the Moslem Caliphate at bay for nearly two decades of its autonomous existence. Why is knowledge of this so obscured in the annals of the African peoples? This lacuna must occupy central space in other dedicated narratives. Those of us who are or were once students of history, or have remained simply engrossed in the fortunes of our ancestors throughout the world, including pan-Africanists of all colors and contours, have been so west-oriented that the history of the African Diaspora remains limited to contact with European intruders. Thus, it is always handier to recall the attempt of Napoleon to reimpose slavery on the Haitian colony in 1804, and his defeat at the hands of a slave army of the African people under the leadership of Jacques Desallines. The dispersal of Africans throughout the Arab world, by contrast, the fate of their cultures and their social status in the Arabized parts of the continent and the Middle East, remains as yet a largely hidden chapter, yet that very history has assumed a tragic immediacy in parts of the black continent.

We must home in on a specific, ongoing scenario that yet again instructs or—perhaps one should say—accuses much of humanity of its tragic limitations in the effort to escape the conditioning of history, most of all when it comes to a determination of the rights and dignity of others. We shall not attempt to predict what form of resolution will prevail on the African continent from the most dangerous manifestation of this chronic pathology, the condescending relationship between one racial entity and another—called racism—that much of the world chooses to ignore. Else it is addressed as a remote aberration, or as a "reactionary" interpretation of events by accusing voices that remain mired in illusory classifications of social phenomena, primitivists who cling to a reductionist rendition of economic/class disparities, etc., etc. These are all seductive, high-sounding ploys of dismissal, but they are pat, partial, and escapist.

The race upheavals of increasing virulence in Zanzibar, Mauritania, and elsewhere in the past four decades and, most lately, and on an unprecedented scale, in the Sudan, warn that the doctrine of revisionism by concealment or elision merely postpones the day of reckoning. Yes, indeed, the border war of 1989 between Senegal and Mauritania may have been precipitated by a contest for water resources or grazing land. However, is there wisdom in denying other contributory factors, such as a history of poor management of evident racial tensions, or the fact that the estimated 75,000 citizens expelled from Mauritania were nearly totally of the black African definition? Concealment or denial encourages the tendency of repetition in those whom this benefits, and with ever increasing confidence in impunity. Was Darfur enabled, even made thinkable, by the school of historic elision? Even as Mauritania was a northwestward destination of the slave commodity from the west coast, Sudan, after all, was a supply depot of the trans-Saharan and Red Sea slave crossings. Certainly, a complacent existence and conduct within the Sudan's past conditioning must be recognized, since there is no pressure, no inducement to redress it. It is short-changing the power of history to pretend that the events in the Sudan are not based on a perception that dates back to a relationship rooted in the history of slavery, even without the words of Koichiiro Matsuura, past secretary-general of UNESCO, who called attention to the continent's own share in "the particularity of this tragedy, and its "*'persisting consequences for modern societies.'*" This is the practical lesson for the moral imperative that is deeply embedded in the mission statement of UNESCO as it embarked on its Slave Route project: "to break the silence surrounding the slave trade and slavery."

It would seem that the American president Bill Clinton, during his time in office, discerned a need for some process toward closure within the society over which he presided, thus his attempts to redress history's unsavory past. His gesture in recalling the notorious Tuskegee syphilis experiment was a remarkable exercise, remarkable in that there appeared to have been no immediate cause for it, no event that triggered the recollection of that dark American past and the need for rethinking its history. In addition to rehabilitating the hanged witches of Salem—a three-hundred-year history, and the subject of Arthur Miller's play *The*

Crucible—Clinton apologized for the Tuskegee syphilis experiment that used the African-Americans as guinea pigs without their knowledge of the actual course of the experiments. That is, they were injected with the syphilis virus, but treatment was withheld from some of them—one of the most diabolical events in medical scientific research on this side of the Equator. Such disposable human material was of course none other than the progeny of slaves—in short, hereditary property. Bill Clinton followed his journey through historic remorse while on African soil, by coming quite close to an apology for the slave trade. Was he playing politics? It hardly matters. The motivating factor for these "revisions of history"—one positive face of historic revisionism—goes beyond attempting to close the account books of the past. In fact, they do anything but close the accounts—they reopen the obscured ledger sheets of reckoning, thus serving as a potential critique, perhaps a restraining factor in present and future human designs. These may be considered arguments in favor of reparations, but this is not our purpose here.

Clinton's gesture of rectifying the errors of history has also been matched in Asia—the Japanese were dragged to the confessional altar, made to express remorse for their crimes against the Korean people, the sexual enslavement (again that word, that sub-humanizing condition) of Korean women, known as military comfort women, sacrificial brides to the Shinto gods. And finally, to bring us closer to the present: at the approach of the bicentennial anniversary of the abolition of the slave trade in all British possessions, in 2008, the prime minister of Great Britain, Tony Blair, came as close as Bill Clinton to an apology to the African peoples for the role of the British in the trade in human flesh.

Interestingly, critics among his own people insisted that he did not go far enough, that he did not express a clear-cut apology; others stridently claimed that there was nothing over which to apologize. Apology or not, anniversaries are convenient occasions for confronting the past. To make their derivatives quite explicit: confrontation with history may enable us to "escape its conditioning"—that is, a conditioning that comes from a history of skewed human relationships—enables humanity to "fly off its seemingly magnetized trajectory into a new orbit of mutual human recognition and respect."

I began by admitting my occasionally ambiguous relationship with ritual. Here now is an instance of a positive use—or adaptation—of ritual proceeding.

On November 11, 2006, a rather quaint ritual took place in a hall on the third floor of a building directly opposite the headquarters of the United Nations, in New York. Because of its location, and the height of the floor, that ritual was played out against a background of the United Nations flags fluttering across the street through the window of the hall. It took the form of a judicial trial and I was the unlikely presiding judge, the event being to try the leader of an African nation accused of crimes against humanity. Yes, it was a form of playacting, but it was a deadly serious one, conducted in all solemnity. Witnesses had been flown to New York for that purpose—aid workers, outside observers, journalists who had barely escaped becoming casualties themselves, but above all, direct victims and survivors, some of whom were still undergoing counseling for their ensuing trauma. Some of them choked up, others could not hold back tears as they testified, relieving days and weeks of anguish all over again.

It was a ritual—the facts were already known, and no pretense was made otherwise, even as we formally appointed internationally reputable lawyers for the absent accused, the Sudanese government, which had predictably ignored the invitation sent through its New York embassy. The panel of judges included a member who had visited Sudan on several occasions at the head of her charitable organization for the relief of the Fur women, and had personally interacted with hundreds of victims of the abused. I had not visited, but it was not for want of trying.

2006 was a year when, for several months, one single event dominated the international media in virtually every corner of the globe, to the almost complete exclusion of any other happening on the globe. It was a period that rivaled the media effect of the long-running murder trial saga of O. J. Simpson. Even the war in Iraq faded into obscurity. Mugabe used the global eclipse of attention to accelerate his demolition of a few more urban settlements that still proved stubborn strongholds of opposition to his despotic rule . . . and so on and on.

The event that overwhelmed the media, however, almost to the exclusion of every other media-worthy happening on the globe, was the uproar over cartoons of Prophet Mohammed published by a notoriety-seeking editor of some obscure journal in a provincial Danish town. This incident, of seemingly apocalyptic dimension, drove into obscurity another event that was taking place simultaneously, impacting irreversibly on the lives of some two and a half to three million people: the genocidal onslaught on Darfur. This ongoing crime against humanity crumpled into fragmentary corners of the international media. Under cover of a global hysteria, the Sudanese government continued to break every undertaking it had given the world for the control of the latest band of *génocidaires* on the African continent, a militia known as the Janjaweed. Instead, it became hyperactive in its "cleansing" agenda; the world went into a coma.

There were, as always, the exceptions here and there. A new initiative by the Elie Wiesel Foundation for Humanity—which had only recently returned from a mission to Aceh, in the victim heartland of the Indonesian tsunami—was tabled, this time, in the direction of Darfur. I had no hesitation in accepting to be part of that mission, convinced that if the victims had been offered a choice between the visitation of the tsunami's inundating waves and the serial waves of violence of the so-called Janjaweed, they would have preferred the kinder onslaught of the tsunami. In my BBC Reith lectures, in the section that dealt with Power and Dignity, I make that straightforward distinction—the power that is unleashed by nature's forces, however destructive or devastating, never humiliates or degrades, but that exercised by one human being over another, or by a section of humanity over another, is the very expression of contempt, humiliation, and disdain.

Our mission to Darfur was scheduled for April 3 to 7. I equipped myself with a small video recorder, determined to bring back live testimonies, in the unlikely event that the Sudanese government did live up to its assurances and permitted us free movement and contacts, especially during projected visits to refugee camps. High-level visitations,

such as those of Colin Powell, former U.S. secretary of state, and Kofi
Annan, secretary-general of the U.N., had already established the progression of yet another sordid chapter of impunity before which the
world appeared helpless to act. Alas, the cries of the African populace in adversity tend to take a back seat in whatever global audiences are formed
before the chambers of redress. As for our mission, the not so unpredictable occurred, as tersely worded in the following communiqué from the
Elie Wiesel Foundation. This "Letter to the Editor" was published in the
New York Times shortly after that newspaper had carried a news item on
the Sudanese government's denial of entry to a U.N. official:

> Re "Sudan Blocks U.N. Official from Visiting Darfur Re-
> gion" (news article, April 4, 2006)
> The Elie Wiesel Foundation for Humanity planned a del-
> egation to Darfur this week as part of its Nobel Laureates
> Initiative. But the government of Sudan told us that permis-
> sion to enter the country was under review.
> Elie Wiesel, the 1986 Nobel Peace Prize recipient, has
> sent the following message to the Darfur Coalition, which
> is organizing a rally in Washington on April 30:
> "In Darfur, humankind's center of suffering today, men,
> women, and children are uprooted, starved, tortured, muti-
> lated, humiliated, and massacred—and the whole civilized
> world knows it. And little or nothing significant is being
> done to stop these massive violations of human rights. Who
> is guilty? Those who commit these crimes. But to the ques-

tion, "Who is responsible," we are compelled to say: "Aren't we all?"

From the last century, the bloodiest in human history, we must take at least one lesson. Those who commit genocide cannot hide behind national borders and claims of sovereignty. There is no choice but to act in defense of defenseless people.

Yes, indeed, we were all set to go. Assurances had been given, visa formalities completed, I had canceled engagements—as I am certain others had—when the Sudanese government developed cold feet. I do not know if the U.N. was offered any reason for the prohibition of its official, but ours was that preparations for the Arab League Summit due to take place shortly were already in high gear, and would conflict with the visit of three or four Nobel laureates to the heart of the landmass of the largest country in Africa. Perhaps it was just as well—one should always look on the bright side. We could have been provided visas only to find that we had traveled all that distance to be confined to a five-star hotel in Khartoum or herded out to spend time among the undoubtedly fascinating monuments that litter the Sudanese landscape—but far from Darfur. We knew how these things work—escort gone missing, sudden "escalation" of hostilities rendering the route dangerous, minister trapped in cabinet meetings, and of course an insistence on first welcoming and updating us in person, etc., etc.

The Arab League Summit did not take place until months after our botched visit. We did not receive any consoling news that the surrogate arm of the Sudanese government, the Janjaweed Arab raiders, had announced a cease-fire in honor of the summit. Instead, each new day brought reports of renewed acts of the Janjaweed progression in its unhidden—indeed, loudly trumpeted—goal of the "arabization" of indigenous African peoples, land, and history, with all its attendant violence and eradication of black African racial identity.

What images I would have brought back, if any, would probably have contributed only to the dulling of the mind, a numbing of its capacity for further retention and/or assessment of man's capacity for evil. The average mind tends to protect itself from overload by developing a resistance to these reminders, which is perhaps why they continue to occur, and with increasing impunity. Sudan continued to manifest herself, in all crude, boastful manner, as a worthy successor to the vanquished Apartheid theology of South Africa.

The infamous publication that riveted most of the attention of the world made one question the designation of Man as a proponent of the activity of reason. I had, as readily admitted, my own personal agenda. We already possessed images of the dehumanization of Sudanese black indigenes, but I had set my sights on obtaining my own first-hand images, then, at debriefing sessions, projecting them side by side with the cartoons, already proliferating on the Internet, that gave such offence, then inviting my audiences to compare—just as an exercise in humanistic reckoning—the all-consuming frenzy over one act of boorishness and insensitivity by a little-known editor in the arctic wastes, with the whimpers that were conceded over Darfur at the time—and only occasionally at that—from global conscience, whimpers that were no sooner teased out than they were nearly smothered by the sheer ponderousness of corresponding inaction. For the cartoons, by contrast, all other global business appeared to have come to a halt. Diplomatic notes flew across the globe between national and religious leaders, embassies battened down their hatches, state of alert "advisories" bombarded travelers, the Security Council held emergency sessions, torrid statements of disavowal filled airwaves and international media, messages of sympathy, of hurt, of solidarity, threats of religious war, of Armageddon, Huntingdon, Fukuyama, and Mahapralaya . . . and in the meantime, what was happening in Darfur?

Now here is a testimony regarding a regular occurrence, with hundreds if not thousands of like reports to be found in compilations by U.N. officials. This came from an interview with one of the survivors.

Hundreds of armed men mounted on camels and horses attacked the town of Tawila on the Eastern slope of Jebel Marra, the heart of the Fur lands. By the time the attack was over, three days later, 75 people had been killed, 350 women and children abducted and more than 100 women raped including 41 teachers and girls from Tawila boarding school. Six of the women were raped in front of their fathers, who were then killed: some of them were gang-raped.

No, that specific incident did not take place during the cartoon brouhaha but a full year earlier. It formed part of the testimonies of a current nature that we had hoped to update on our mission, with the victims speaking directly into the camera or recorder, having set in motion an independent machinery for encounters with witnesses to similar raids. The opportunity was denied, as one has learned to expect.

Darfur is of tragic cooperation in delimiting the many areas that usually complicate such conflicts. Both violators and victims are followers of the same religion and thus, mercifully, one element, and a very emotive one, as illustrated by the cartoon episode, had been eliminated. The line of demarcation of sides in the Sudan has been largely drawn along other parameters. Prominent among these of course was—and still is—race. Once again, there is no shortage of self-indicting evidence for this attribution.

Sources, including documents retrieved by U.N. inspectors and observers from the headquarters of a Sheik Musa Hilal, leader of the notorious Janjaweed, reinforced by pronouncements of Sudanese parliamentarians, local governors, military operational orders, and intercepted exchanges between Sudanese military pilots in their bombing sorties on defenseless villages, have painted an unambiguous picture of the Sudanese government's systematic pogrom of the region of Darfur, a policy that was being prosecuted beyond any ambiguity through the already mentioned Janjaweed raiders, the Arabist militia that was raised, funded, and armed by the Sudanese government and directed by its military and intelligence services. Long before the pivotal visits by Kofi Annan and Colin Powell, a number of enterprising journalists had designated a crime against humanity that was already in progress, directed largely at the African indigenes of Darfur. They had filed reports on this wide-scale, violent denial of the indigenous African people's right to existence.

The Human Rights organization CREDO, a fully African-founded and -staffed initiative, had been battering at the doors of the African Union with compelling evidence for years, hounding African leaders at their interminable gatherings and into their own home stations, urging strong action for the relief of the Western Sudanese. The then-chairman of the African Union Commission, Oumar Konare, had paid several visits to the country and the refugee camps—his commitment went beyond mere formal responsibilities. He held meetings with Sudanese officials from Omar Bashir downward. I was in a position to know, directly from him, that his condemnation of the Sudanese government was unequivocal. Lacking, however, was the will of the leaders of African member states to activate their forces for practical intervention on an effective, not tokenist, scale.

The facts were known, the trial was strictly ritual, and, yes, unanimously and predictably, the panel found the defendant, General Omar Bashir of Sudan, guilty as charged. It was a symbolic act, designed to trigger awake the designated structural engineers of an ideal world order, the U.N. clan, who remained trapped in the gilded web of rhetoric and protocols, bargaining and doubletalk, while the greatest crime against humanity on the African continent since the killing spree of Rwanda was taking place, right under their gaze. What is sometimes served for dessert in the U.N. restaurants and cafeterias is so easy to discern—it is fruits specially flown in from the Ouidah Tree of Forgetfulness.

Those who wish to understand the undercurrents of the mind that breed and nurture the inhuman conduct of the Sudanese government against sections of its own populace, notably now the peoples of

Western Sudan, the Fur, would do well to take good note of the role of history in this scenario. It is totally superfluous that the favorite battle-cry, as abundantly testified by survivors of the Janjaweed marauders in their mission of ethnic cleansing, has been none other than that historic cry of disdain: "Kill the slaves!" The Ku Klux Klan, night riders of the American Deep South, had a similar cry: "Hang the niggers!" That ex-hortation has been recorded in numerous testimonies, including at the New York tribunal, and will surely feature in the sealed indictments that the United Nations finally executed a year later—"Kill the slaves"—and variants thereof. The yet unexpiated history of the trans-Sahara slave trade, that is, the centuries-old history of the relationship between two races on the African continent, has coalesced into a master-slave tradi-tion, one that establishes one part of the population as its subhuman sector, subject to permanent humiliation through neglect, double stan-dards of governance, uneven application of the law, and enthronement of impunity, leaving such a sector prone to elimination if and whenever it insists on a revision of its social status. African-Americans who find it difficult to make a transposition of their sensibilities to the landscape of Darfur should simply revert to their own not-so-distant history, vestiges of which still dominate the conduct of one race toward another and erupt from time to time. Like the Korean "comfort women," or the black victims of the lynch sport and the Tuskegee syphilis experiment, the people of Darfur remain object possessions in the minds of the rul-ing class of Sudan, who pride themselves as Arabs and suzerains. Often indistinguishable in complexion, bound together by the same religion, the violators nonetheless view themselves as beings of a slave-owning pedigree, a distinction that takes its authority from none other than the consistently obscured, evaded, or deodorized history of pre-European (Arab) slave commerce on the African continent.

Not that slavery, even in its formal sense, is extinct on the continent. Quite apart from truckloads of child slaves that are still rescued by the police en route to uncertain destinations in my own Nigeria and other West African states—read Uwem Akpan's *Say You Are One of Them*—we know that more than mere vestiges of slavery exist, for instance, in today's Mauritania. That relationship was responsible for the massacre of some hundred soldiers twenty years ago—these incidents are ill-reported even in the foreign press—and that relationship also accounts for the massacre of about three times the same number of civilians in that same country *three* years after an uprising within the military, and led to the earlier-mentioned expulsion of Senegalese indigenes from the country. It is that history of the vestigial slave relationship that manifests itself so cynically and brutally in today's Sudan. It forms more than a mere backdrop to the civil war that raged in that nation for more than three decades, devastating much of civil society and cultures in Southern Sudan. That front was eventually pacified through mutual attrition and the unbroken will of resistance, and the humiliated Sudanese government transferred its frustrations to Western Sudan, to the region known as Darfur. These ongoing master-slave encounters are cynically disguised in official communiqués from within and without— one recalls how the United Nations shied away from employing the word "genocide" in reporting the Rwandan massacres. Still, disguise it how we choose, these unexorcised relations, and their contestation by the second half of that deadly coupling—master and slave—reveal the psychopathology of the actors in the Darfur tragedy.

That yet subsisting pathology of the slave owner is memorably captured in an anecdote recounted by the Nigerian author Kole Omotoso in his reprise of Nigerian history, *Just Before Dawn*. Omotoso was writing about that phase in West African history when the movement for the abolition of the slave trade finally got under way—from whatever motivations, commercially convenient, altruistic, or a mixture of both. A British colonial officer attempted to lecture an emir—a traditional ruler in Northern Nigeria—on the British resolve to end the trade. It riled that potentate beyond endurance, causing him to explode: "Can you tell a cat to stop mousing? I shall die with a slave in my mouth!"

To that emir, to the slavemaster of the American Deep South and West Indies, sections of humanity remain property, and ownership confers authority to dispose of one's own items as wishes—brand, amputate, castrate, rape, hang, or eat them. Like Napoleon, who traduced the Age of Enlightenment in order to re-enslave the nation of Haiti, like the thrill killers of the USA who dragged a living body tied to the back of their trucks and, literally, flayed him alive, like these and thousands more unrecorded examples, the Sudanese government continued to defy the laws of humanity, the United Nations, and indeed its African peer governments, taunting—"Mind your own business. This is a sovereign state, one that must be left alone to exercise its prerogative of ownership over its human possessions."

This is the only reality that has resulted in over two hundred thousand dead, victims as much of indiscriminate aerial bombardment as of state-supported marauding gangs, placing two and a half million human beings in makeshift tents, prey not only of the dry desert wind, of drought and disease, but of the marauding horse and camel riders of the Janjaweed, the Ku Klux Klan of Darfur. They ride out to pillage even the scanty rags of these dispossessed people, even in refugee camps beyond the Sudanese borders, confident not only of the protection of, but basking in, the propulsive complicity of the government. It was this reality that emboldened the Sudanese government to camouflage—at least as recorded up to 2007—its military planes with the colors and emblem of the United Nations as it imported tons and tons of arms into the beleaguered area, in defiance of the Security Council's injunctions and its own agreements, and right under the noses of U.N. observers. That exercise continued even into the ritual trial of General Omar Bashir in New York. It is that history that makes the government proclaim, in black and white, its mission to "arabize" the entire Sudanese landscape, which of course necessitates the eradication of other indigenous cultures and the extermination of its peoples. Once again, the word, the avoidance word that remained missing in U.N. resolutions, was genocide.

The emir's tale is not apocryphal, and it mercifully speaks of a largely extinct species, transplanted and/or reactivated through a time warp into the Sudan. The orders that the Sudanese government has given its storm troopers, the incontinent Janjaweed, for its Final Solution, as it arms them with the very latest weaponry and logistical support from special military detachments, are precisely the sentiments of that emir: "Ride out—and return with a few dozen slaves in your mouth." The Janjaweed have followed that exhortation to the letter, and some.

This is what the world, but most accusingly, the African continent itself failed for so long to understand. This is what the Arab League family, of which Sudan is a prominent member, refuses to acknowledge, thus failing to discipline its errant member—indeed, has conducted itself in blatant encouragement of Bashir's career of impunity, along with its quislings in the African Union, even to the extent of rejecting the United Nations' indictment of the defiant dictator for crimes against humanity. By contrast, the forceful intervention of that league in the Libyan and Syrian uprisings, on behalf of its fellow Arab citizens, sets the seal on its comparative human regard that requires no further commentary! This is why the conscience of the African continent, the staging ground of the much-vaunted African Renaissance, has gone into a prolonged harmattan sleep, slumped around the Tree of Forgetfulness. The very notion is mind-boggling, an insolent ordination of the mangy catechism of impunity, that while the rest of the world—the Japanese, the Europeans, the Americans, and possibly now, haltingly, the Turks—is redressing history, commemorating the termination of a shameful past, expressing remorse for such a past in other parts of the world, the very opposite, an atavistic assertiveness, is in the ascendant on the African continent in the twenty-first century. A ruling, exultantly racist cabal elevates that same shaming history to a principle of racial pride and mobilizes its bandits to consolidate historic iniquities. In the hundreds of thousands, today's slave catchers are still overrunning ancient settlements, burning crops, slaughtering cattle, poisoning wells, raping mothers in front of their own children and husbands, girl pupils in front of their teachers, fathers, and mothers, pulverizing villages and eradicating cultures, unrepentant riders of night and day defiant of world censure. They ride off in total confidence of immunity, in full glare of the world's searchlights, with—literally—hundreds of slaves in their mouths.

It is preferable, more dignified, that Africa should refuse to matter if such reckoning-with can be attained only in a negative mode—on account of international derelictions. Her humanity—for this is what continents or nations are primarily made of, without this they are meaningless—deserves better than to earn its right to existence from serving as a prod for the conscience of the world. It is far too heavy a price to pay for the role of resurrecting world memory, evoking the challenges of past failures and the pledges that formed the foundation and pillars of a new world order. "Never again," after all, was the pledge that followed Auschwitz and Belsen. "Never again," read the United Nations' ritual resolve after Yugoslavia and Rwanda. Perhaps, in keeping with such ritual pronouncements, to acknowledge the triumph of Rites and Ritual over Rights and Redress, yes, if only as a footnote to that Ritual played against the flags of all nations that many read as ensigns of the Rights of Humanity, that intervening space, now known as the U.N. Plaza, should be renamed the Never Again Plaza. It would be more than appropriate, even prophetic, since we shall undoubtedly be lulled yet again into a state of inertia by those two words of numbing predictability, landscaped into the accommodating earth of the African continent, draped around the sole surviving growth in the Darfurian wasteland—the Tree of Forgetfulness—a sturdy, ironic emblem that places the future in denial all over again with the world's unfulfilled promise: Never again!

PART II *Body and Soul*

5. A Choice of Chains

Most depressingly of all, the persistent denial of the fruits of liberation which must be an affirmation of human equality through a respect for rights and dignity, voice and volition—it is this social reality across African populations that generates a feeling of hopelessness and impotence, evoking a past in cyclic recurrence—in short, the image of a continent re-enslaved.

Millennium Commission report, 2001

AS IF THE CONTINENT DID NOT HAVE enough on her plate, enter a shadowy but lethal force determined to reenslave a continent with its chains of fundamentalist theology! The despotic spirit of the secular—demonstrated since independence by much of African brutal leadership—now confronts its theocratic rival, leaving the populace prostrate under twin self-proclaimed orders of salvation. Alas, failure to choose is the worst of choices. Between fundamentalist ruthlessness and secular excess there is not really much of a dilemma, and it is a choice that matters, not just to the African continent but even more crucially to the rest of the world. While secular dictatorship can be confronted at various stages, the testimony of history is that the chains placed around the mind through religious absolutism are far more constrictive, tenacious, and implacable than those of their secular counterparts. To be under orders of an identifiable entity leaves the door open for negotiations, even of a lop-sided nature. When such orders are attributed to an invisible or centuries-dead authority, however, transmitted through intermediaries who insist that they are only "carrying out orders" but have appropriated access to the Sole Authoritative Voice that dispenses such orders, all dialogue is foreclosed.

Heirs to African thought systems and world-views are, however, equipped with antecedent traditions that enable a repudiation of both, make them capable of that liberating response, "A plague on both your houses!"—pronounced first in the direction of the rivaling dictatorships of secular and theocratic ideologies and, next, as a rejection of the aggressively twinned agencies of the latter, the theocratic—Christianity and Islam. The earlier named arm of the binaries of rejection—secular despotism—has engendered its own brutal civil wars and cost millions of lives and decades in development, as African facilitators of western and eastern interests sought to entrench themselves in power, invoking the mission of one ideological bloc or the other, sometimes in rapidly alternating allegiances. This was the epoch of the mythology of the "strong leader," a trumpeted sine qua non for a continent of presumed infantilism. The more brutal to his own people but subservient to outside interests—forget the bluster and posturing!—the more tightly embraced and lavishly enabled each has proved: Idi Amin, Bokassa, Mobutu, Said

Barre, and all. The geography of that phase is much contracted, the tendency measurably attenuated under the banner of democracy. The so-called Arab Spring, dramatic as it has been in spread and tempo, did not commence in the Arab world but on African soil, and it germinated decades before the Tunisian uprising, almost coterminous with the very unfurling of the flag of independence.

And now, the *renewed*—for this must always be borne in mind—*renewed* claims of the other "House," the self-proclaimed Dwelling of God whose partisans march with scripture in one hand and Kalashnikov or suicide bomb in the other, all remain oblivious or indifferent to the archaic nature of millennia-old, primitive impulses that periodically erupt and devastate swathes of the world since the marriage of religion to the naked agenda of power. The physical warring ground for theocratic dominance over the secular could easily have been any one of several of Africa's vulnerable underbellies—it only happens today to be Somalia and the Horn of Africa. That region is eminently qualified, however, being long in gestation, little acknowledged but with audible stirrings and periodic explosions. Where it suited him, Colonel Qaddafi, who dreamed of being King of Africa but met the ignominious end of a "sewer rat," never hesitated to stir the lethal broth with lavish financing, alliances, and even open declarations of purpose—theocracy and secular rhetoric of the radical kind being mere optional gloves over his fist of power. The resolve of the African Union to stem the tide of the theocratic power thrust in Somalia therefore constitutes a far-reaching stage of decisiveness, not only through its recognition of the more secularly inclined Somalian government of 2009, but by its approval of an interventionist force. The decision behind Ethiopia's unilateral incursion into Somalia, in support of the interim government, was certainly controversial, but that only raised the primary question: Who was—and still is—the primary interloper on African soil? The government of Ethiopia, or the borderless quasi-government known as al-Qaeda? Whichever way that question is eventually resolved, hopefully not as a verbal exercise but in the spirit of Abidjan, where the decision was taken to sustain the interim government formed from warring sides, the future of that tortured land, Somalia, remains filled with foreboding. The Horn of Africa bleeds again, profusely.

It is useful to interject at this point a reminder that the continent of Africa has refused to remain bounded by her geographical saltwater borders. This was a consequence, obviously, of the intervention of outsiders, but then that intervention has taken off on a life of its own, its products accepting their irreversible destiny as the matured transformation of seeds transplanted in alien soil. Fairly adjusted in the main, though still far from fully integrated, grown, despite that lack, in confidence and capabilities, certainly in full cognizance of the world's complexities, those forced exiles began to turn for identification, or structured concern, toward their continent of origin. Like the rest of the world, they were not immune from the consciousness of universal stock-taking that overtakes a people at the approach of any epoch of significance, such as the commencement of a new century—a fin de siècle impulsion that manifests itself even more compellingly at a millennial notation such as the world celebrated in 2000, the year that instigated the U.N.-sponsored Millennial Commission for Africa. A hundred years earlier, for the Diaspora African, that centennial spirit was evident in the seizure and replacement of the tentative, largely tokenist awakening of a European conscience to the inhumanity of slavery, the replacement of its pietisms with concrete proposals for the future of its victims who now spoke forcibly in their own voice. Descendants of that massive displacement began to insert into their own emancipation agenda the Big Question Mark: What future for a vast continent that had undergone such a massive cardiac arrest? It is instructive to consider, in our earlier specified context, how prescient they were.

For instance, in 1900, spearheaded by the West Indian lawyer Sylvester Williams and attended by delegates from Ethiopia, Sierra Leone, Liberia, and Gold Coast (to become Ghana at independence), an exploratory conference of African descendants set the stage in London. Between that centennial notation and the Second World War, a number of offshoots followed—1919, 1921, 1923—in Brussels, Paris, London, then the 1945 Congress in Manchester. In between were several gatherings, of varied dimensions, including within the United States. By then the intellectual and political vision of Africa had broadened with the entry of figures such as George Padmore, another West Indian, the American sociologist W. E. B. Du Bois, and later, from the continent itself, Kwame Nkrumah, Jomo Kenyatta, and their peers. To these leaders of political thought, Africa did not merely matter, she was all that mattered.

Artistes and intellectuals as a self-identifying group were not left behind in the projected shaping of the continent, resolved that the future of this landmass should not be left only to politicians, even of the fiery nationalist mold. Paris, Italy, and London played host to a number of African and Diaspora thinkers and writers—Richard Wright, Léopold Sédar Senghor, Nicolás Guillén, Aimé Césaire, Jean Price-Mars, Rabemananjara, Birago and David Diop, among others. As the debates demonstrated, they were spurred on additionally by the new Question Mark on European humanism that lay in rubble after two wars and the Holocaust. These urged a separation and reinterrogation of African values, as an independent human tributary long suppressed and/or denigrated by a world whose own claims to superiority had become severely undermined. Barbarisms that stemmed from its internal and external contradictions had seen to this—evidence of the latter provided by exposures of European conduct in their colonies. After a war of fratricidal savagery, that dominant entity, Europe, was also resituating herself, thus providing for the descendants of the African continent an active backdrop against which to direct their own emergence as a distinct people. The rise of communism was an additional spur to a thorough overhaul of western ideas, offering options on the very nature of societal evolution and construct. The African continent was approached by a number of these thinkers as a tabula rasa—after all it was, in a sense, in a state of suspended animation. Freed from the "ideology" of the west, one that had proved so negative in her history, Africa was slipping her umbilical cord, ready to be scribbled upon from base without the baggage of increasingly suspect teaching. By the 1945 conference, the word "socialism" was taking its place side by side with self-governance.

That recognition of Africa as an entity in need of definition and direction was thus not a post-independence phenomenon. It began when the very notion of independent African states was unthinkable. It became qualitatively charged and differently orientated only during and after the struggle for independence and the challenges of national affirmation, taking on an accelerated tempo. Thus the complex brainstorming sessions, further complicated by the contest between the ideological blocs, east and west. The leaders of the anticolonial generation confronted specific problem issues of a continent poised to enter a modern world order, excited by the very consciousness of an inchoate, nearly amorphous burden but definitely palpable in its promise, not only for the communities then in formation, but for the rest of the world. Africa began to take shape as an entity that demanded visionary planning, provoked comparisons with other national units of widely different or similar beginnings, such as Indonesia, Malaysia, and Singapore. Eventually those nations of a shared colonial origin would constitute a silent or vociferous rebuke, still cited today, since they rapidly moved far ahead of their sibling nations on the African continent. Despite such chastening mirrors, however, for the more theologically inclined, and for an emerging breed of scholars and poets, Africa remained proof of the definite existence of a "mystic portion of creation" that had displayed, once in a forgotten past, the authentic soul of humanity. It was an entity that would blaze forth eventually as a redemptive destination always close to hand, the exorcising of an intervening "curse," fulfilling, in Edward Blyden's words, "the divinely mandated mission of the retrieval of a Paradise Lost."

And here we come to the crucial and pertinent lesson. Deeply steeped, as we can see, in Christian upbringing, as were the leaders of the slave descendants—like nearly all the slave population of the western

world—it is hardly surprising that their language of African retrieval was
mostly couched in Christian metaphors, just as the venues for all the pan-
Africanist meetings, including sponsorship and/or material support,
came from the resources of Christian nations, churches, and missionary
societies. Yet all these encounters, including those that took place on
an American soil of Bible-thumping origins, even to its constitutional
invocations, were marked by a recognition, and an approbation, of the
religious plurality of the world, and thus, a rejection of any imposition
of a national religion for the emerging nations of the African continent.
Among the resolutions adopted at what was titled "The Mass Meeting
of the National Association for the Advancement of Coloured People,
Carnegie Hall"—universally known by its initials, the NAACP—on
January 6, 1919, resolutions for the enabling protocols for the emerging nations of the African Continent, this specific item was moved and
passed under "Culture and Religion":

> No particular religion shall be imposed and no particular
> form of human culture. There shall be liberty of conscience.

Individually and generationally, this gathering of freed slaves understood
bondage. Seeking to establish both their own identity in an alien land,
and reflect the same on the continent of their concern, they took time
off to recognize the perils of imposed religions. Significantly, they were
not even thinking of Islam but of Christianity! This was the religion of
the colonizers, and they recognized that a crucial part of the armory of
domination, of entrenching the actuality of conquest, is the imposition
of the conqueror's religion and culture.

A century later, this time on African soil, a Millennium Commission, embarked on the same project of self-reconstitution, would revert
to the same social ideal and as forcefully, spurred undoubtedly by the
now undeniable counteragenda of religious imperialism that had begun
to charge into the continent, and deplore the obsession of a part to "polarize the world along religious lines." Religious wars have not exactly
begun to rip the continent apart from pole to pole, but the blood-stained
banner of intolerance and imposed conformity has been hoisted, and
deadly probes are daily inserted across the continent, from Mauritania
to the Horn of Africa and in parts in between, including Nigeria. The
word "polarize" is indeed most apt, since it derives from a presumption
of a binary contestation, whereas the anterior reality—pre-Christian,
pre-Islamic—vibrantly present on the continent, disputes this.

Has Africa any lessons to impart to the new imperators of the
religious hegemonic realm, of which Somalia in particular has become a
vicious testing ground? The answer is yes indeed. So let us move then to
examine Africa's spirituality—abandoning with relief the homeopathic
for the therapeutic—and its lessons for the world. Before that, however, a word from a Moslem scholar, one of an increasing vocal number who have exhibited the courage to remind their countrymen and
women that Islam is fundamentally a humanistic, liberating avocation,
and that the invocation of divine authority in the repression of enquiry
and knowledge is what constitutes distortions within the Islamic faith,
whose consequence for society can only be stagnation, and even retar-
dation. There is no escaping, no shying away from the hurtful truth,
though we do insist on precision: Not Islam, but what is now generally
known as Political Islam and its hegemonic aggression has leapt to the

fore as the latest among the destablizing factors that continue to plague the African continent.

Now to Ismail Serageldin, director of the Library of Alexandria, Egypt, who has taken the battle to the theocratic manipulators of the Islamic faith and world-view: His words, in a July 2009 lecture:

> It is my view that we should not invoke or involve religion in matters where judgment is not for theologians but specialists. For such matters are not concerned with what is religiously permitted or prohibited (Halal or Haram) but rather with what is right or wrong and in the interest of the common good; all of which can change in keeping with time, place and circumstances For example, if we decide to set the speed limit for the Cairo-Alexandria road as one-hundred kilometers, this does not imply that 110 km speed would be religiously prohibited and 90 km permitted. Such decisions are based on the type of road, the technology of transportation and road accidents' statistics; all of which are matters for specialists and not for theologians.
>
> This phenomenon of directing every matter, great or small, religious or worldly, to religious scholars for an opinion and a Fatwa is truly surprising. It suspends the use of one's mind, and seeks to transfer the responsibility of the decision— whatever decision—to the originator of the Fatwa. On the other hand, we have learned from our great intellectuals, like Abbas Mahmoud El Akkad, that "applying the mind

is an Islamic duty" and that using your mental faculties is an obligation for all Muslims.

Serageldin—and his school of religious philosophy—could easily have been outlining principles that derive from an African spirituality that predated Islam and Christianity, one, however, that most of the world chose to dismiss as primitive or nonexistent, even though it transferred to the New World, took root in its soil, and permeated the spirituality and cultures of nations like Brazil—and this without aggression or violence, or even overt proselytizing. Earlier, we proposed that Africa stands poised, potentially, on the brink of a new wave of voyages of discovery. If there is one offering that passively waits to irradiate the world with its seminal humanism, it is this offering of the Orisa, one of the "invisible" religions of the African continent.

6. Not a "Way of Life," But a Guide to Existence

FIRST, IT WAS CHRISTIANITY, BUT latterly, and more assertively, Islam, that claims to be a total way of life, encompassing every aspect of human enterprise—ethics, aesthetics, jurisprudence, economics, engineering, healing sciences, etc. Nothing is left to secular intelligence, no human development unforeseen, no attribute unregistered within the provenance of either faith.

My childhood memory of Sunday sermonizing still retains images of a sweaty prelate at the pulpit, laboriously extracting the seeds of several disciplines from selected biblical passages and narratives. His illustrative passage for economics was predictably the parable of a merchant and his three servants to whom he gave different sums before proceeding on a journey. Two traded with their capital and made tidy profits while the third buried his deep in the ground for safekeeping. The last was duly rebuked, while the others received the ultimate approbation in the words—*Well done, thou good and faithful servant, enter thou into the kingdom of the Lord!* The preacher rendered that benediction in such thunderous rapture—his voice echoed round and round the church in such depths of possession—that the words have remained with me till today. As for mathematics, I no longer recall his *quod era demonstran-*

dum, only that it never made a mathematician out of me, and my business aptitude guarantees that I am forever locked out of the kingdom of God.

Decades later, in the nineteen-eighties, it would be the turn of an Islamic cleric/politician to instruct Nigerians in the fundamentals of constitutionalism—the Koran, he declared, was "superior" to the nation's constitution. In lyricism, as inspirational and visionary, he certainly had this writer firmly in his corner—alas, it was not these sublime qualities that our cleric intended. And some time later, when the nation was locked in a debate over whether or not to adopt the IMF's Structural Adjustment Programme, an association of Moslem women, duly instructed, declared authoritatively that the Koran was opposed to it. Most Nigerians were indeed opposed to SAP, but no one that I recall claimed authority from the Bible, the Bhagavad Gita, or the Book of Ifa.

We shall concede a far more modest role for African religions in the lives of African humanity, a role that nonetheless offers a distinct world-view that lays claim to guidance—not dictates!—of its social conduct, human relations, and survival strategies. In response to the holistic, sometimes universalist claims of others, an exegesis of Orisa worship, the millennia-old religion of the West African Yoruba people, more ancient than Islam or Christianity, will attempt to guide us, co-opted befittingly as paradigm for African religions. It survived the Atlantic slave route and sank deep roots in South American and Caribbean spiritual earth. Even where this religion is encountered only on the margins of those societies, it is always with full devotional embrace—including pilgrimages to Source, Ile-Ife, in the land of the Yoruba. Orisa presence embraces Cuba, Dominica, Colombia, parts of the southern United

States, Puerto Rico, Argentina, and, most vibrantly of all—Brazil. At the heart of these displaced cultures will be found the deities, and all the social activities over which they preside—from planting and harvesting to family and clan ethos, technology, historical continuity, from the strategies of communal harmony to the politics of resistance, and, where necessary, even war.

As a frankly seductive strategy, we shall seek our entry point, not even within the mysteries of the religion itself, but in those areas of mundane activities in which religion is implicated, however marginally, making our selection among the more pacific and unavoidable human occupations. The curative sciences—bolstered by their associated lyricism—are as good an entry point as any, serving at the same time as illustration of the "earthiness" of the gods, since health is a common human pursuit, arguably second only to the management of that most basic need for all living species—food. The curative sciences also happen to illustrate the intervention—more accurately integration—of the deities in the basic concerns of humanity, in this instance spelling nothing more mystical than the harmonization of the universe of the human body and mind to the external universe.

The compendium of Ifa, which may be counted the equivalent of the Moslem Koran and Christian Bible, is replete with numerous pronouncements, including ethical precepts, that guide—again, not dictate!—individual and communal choices in virtually all aspects of life. These pronouncements—often in the guise of gnomic observations— make no attempt to regiment the adherents of Orisa. They take no interest in personal matters like dress codes or sexual preferences. Indeed—sacrilege of sacrileges!—to underscore the lack of seriousness in this religion, its "scriptures," the Book of Ifa, actually exhibits a sense of the impish or humorous, sometimes scatological, recognizing that deflation of afflatus is a necessary part of social and spiritual balance and general well-being. Perhaps this is what makes Orisa worship impervious to co-option by the dictatorial priesthood of other religions, who turn mere spiritual intuitions into instruments of repression. Despite the modesty of its spiritual provenance, however, Orisa religion does not hesitate to guide humanity, most especially through Ifa, its compendium of knowledge and paradigmatic narratives.

No religion fails to take an interest in or intrude into secular matters, and Orisa is no exception—but never in a dogmatic vein. Orisa worship, through its scriptures, moves confidently beyond the spiritual or divinatory, engaging issues such as traditional healing and pharmacology in its numerous narratives, set out in verses—the *odu* of Ifa. Belatedly but laudably, UNESCO has admitted the Book of Ifa into its protected series, recognized it as part of what is categorized as the World's Intangible Heritage. For followers, or those merely knowledgeable of Ifa, however, it is not this recognition that lends it validity—very much the contrary. Despite an upbringing of some of us in a Christian environment, the world of the Orisa, fortunately, has provided a tangible backcloth and context of daily existence, often patchily, always palpably. It was a world—formally forbidden—that cast its spell on my childhood imagination, effortlessly carving out a space that it has continued to occupy in its own innate autonomy, but also as a later critique of the competing claims of other world-views, other spiritual claims,

other arrogations of knowledge and truths. Let me introduce here some
formative details of that childhood, which could not have been more
remote from any attempted Orisa conversion.

My mother was what we call a petty trader. Next to her shop was a
traditional healer, a *babalawo,* whose clinic was the verandah of his mud
house, under a lean-to, thus making it quite visible from the frontage
of our own shop, where I often sat. My father was a schoolteacher, and
it struck me that his, and the babalawo's, operations appeared to share
the activity of instruction, so I began to take an illicit interest in his
methods. Illicit because, to a well-brought-up child from a Christian
home, such activities were clearly the work of the devil. Beyond a neigh-
borly good morning, there was hardly any social intercourse between the
healer and our own corner of the block. There was no social ostracism,
as both sides interacted in numerous ways, especially in town affairs and
trade matters, but we, the children, were strictly forbidden to stray in
his direction or play with the children of that household—they were
pagans!

As a child I perhaps suffered from an undiagnosed disease which
manifested itself as compulsive transposition. As narrated in *AKE, The
Years of Childhood*—I was inducted into the church choir—only to be
expected, as I was the son of the headmaster of an Anglican school.
What this meant, however, was that I spent much of the time that was
supposedly taken up with devout church-choiring with viewing, from a
close-up vantage, the full-length portraits of Christian saints and early
missionaries in the stained-glass windows. From my earliest encounter
with these portraits, they morphed constantly into our own *egungun*

(ancestral) "pagan" masquerades, who paraded the streets at festivals, speaking in guttural voices. These were the masquerades of whom Christian missionaries—one of them my own grand-uncle—in their total misconception of the role of these figures in the lives of society, derisively hymned:

> Oh you egungun followers
> Will you kindly stop lying
> He who is dead does not speak
> Oh you egungun followers
> Will you please stop lying. . . .

Moslem preachers were not left far behind in this holy partnership, nor did the Orisa worshippers always remain silent in the face of such provocation, since nothing in Orisa creed enjoins the Christian meekness of "turning of the other cheek." Orisa nonetheless jealously guards— as we shall see—its nonaggressive philosophy. These skirmishes were, however, only of mild, peripheral interest to me, being caught up with the truly mysterious activities that preoccupied our "forbidden"—that is, non-Christian, non-Moslem—neighbor, the babalawo. His activities were certainly mysterious to me, but nothing about them was secretive. His clinic, an open one, was additionally located incongruously across the road from the Anglican church, with its gleaming white tower and sonorous bells that housed the stained-glass windows of saints and missionaries.

The babalawo's method of ministering to patients seemed, at the

beginning, esoteric, compared to the government- and missionary-run
clinics that we normally patronized, yet it did not take too long for me
to begin to detect and voice out (strictly among us sibling delinquents)
certain familiar features of the babalawo's curative methods. They struck
me forcibly as sharing a number of features with the western treatment
at General Hospital, Miss McCutter's prenatal clinic, the Oke Paadi (Padre)
hospital, the Pharmacy, etc., our normal destinations whenever a family
member was taken ill or was about to give birth. As his first step, the
babalawo held consultations; at the end, he dispensed medications—it
all looked like a rite of continuity between the two "worlds." This easy
cohabitation, one that contradicted the actual Christian sermonizing—
separatist in creed and injunctions—was perhaps the single most consistent factor in my elementary comprehension of a lack of absolutely
hermetic spheres that isolate one culture from another. Inevitably, as I
grew older but remained impressionable, this would evolve into a recognition that the coincidence of a number of social principles, usages,
mores—minor or profound—was simply part of a sensory network for a
full appreciation of natural phenomena and their derivatives, including
social practices.

The babalawo's clinic was the place for a more fascinating array of
herbal concoctions dispensed for various illnesses—potions from barks
and roots, bitter and astringent, oily and/or gritty, not too dissimilar
from those that were dispensed by the bottle and spoon in western hospitals. I was also able to observe that the babalawo's consulting shack
was patronized by practicing Christians and Moslems—a number of
them sneaking in after dusk or in the early morning on their way to

white-collar duties. My own Christian family did not patronize our neighbor, unlike my grandfather in his hometown of Isara. He swore by his babalawo. My superimposing eyes also remarked that, in our own home, apart from the pills and potions dispensed from the government hospitals, there were also jars, clay pots, and gourds whose contents were suspiciously like the ones I saw being provided by the babalawo. They gave off more pungent smells, though I never did encounter a more nauseating smell and consistency than the cenapodium, or castor oil, that came from the western clinic. Even more curious was the fact that the barks and roots that stayed within jars from which we were dosed at home for worms, fevers, stomach cramps, and so on were constantly being replenished from allied sources—in short, the babalawo's pharmacopia appeared to alternate or cohabit with the western-issued pills for the same line of afflictions.

My grandfather—then a diehard "pagan" before his questionable conversion—lived in another town, and I soon discerned that his visits also contributed to the home's alternative "first-aid box." He kept the medicine vessels replenished, sometimes sending in fresh barks, roots, and leaves. And occasionally there were incantations to be recited before dosage. Of even greater interest were the sessions held by my father, his colleagues, and their peers over the efficacy of one *agbo*—a prophylactic potion—or another. I watched them share roots, barks, jars of concentrates, discussing their relative virtues.

One deduction emerged effortlessly from those childhood experiences: a distinction between the passive and the active (participatory) curative methods. When I claim that the latter represents a founding

principle of African traditional medicine, I do not thereby limit this to
the African and probably some Asian traditions, but remind us that this
also used to be part of the traditional healing methods of the European
peoples, now vitiated through competitive modern theories and clinical approaches to disease, rivaling interests of corporate pharmaceutical
mega-companies and the so-called scientific methodology. The "return
to source" with the full collaboration of western-trained doctors, is,
however, making strides, perhaps propelled more by commercial stakes than
conviction, but that return is on, and with full vengeance—Chinese,
Thai, Native American, Hawaiian, Scottish, Welsh, and, in increasing
numbers, indeed akin to a new Scramble for Africa—untapped resources
from the Dark Continent!

The babalawo's clinic intrigued me far more than the starched,
white-overall western clinics, where a most impressive looking doctor
hung a stethoscope around his neck, listened to heartbeats, took pulses,
and wrote down prescriptions in indecipherable script. He looked in-
timidatingly omniscient, and he clearly was in touch with all the dialects
of the human body. The babalawo also exuded knowledge and mystery,
but somehow he appeared closer to his patients. For a start, he sat cross-
legged on a floormat and appeared to consult his patient as much as they
consulted him. Here was the process that I observed:

When the patient arrived—let us say a woman—she placed herself
on the floor, opposite the babalawo. Between them was the divination
board, dusted with a kind of whitish flour. I was too far off to follow
what they said to each other—I have of course since studied the entire
process in some detail—but what I observed then was that she took out
a coin, or a personal object, sometimes a cowrie shell. On his instruc-

tions, the suppliant whispered to it, then laid it down at the edge of the board. It was definitely a whisper, intended—again, to be discovered as an adult—as intimate communication between the divination forces and the suppliant, and it was not heard by the babalawo.

The babalawo then proceeded to cast the *opele*—the divination chain—several times, making a set of marks on the board. At the end of a series of casting he looked at the pattern of the marks before him, then recited a verse from Ifa. Sometimes the suppliant shook her head, and then the process was repeated until the suppliant nodded affirmation. The significant factor was that the babalawo made the suppliant an active participant in the process that led to her own diagnosis and prescriptions. Within that process, the most impressively mysterious appeared to be the role played by what sounded like magical incantations. These, I would come to learn, were verses from Ifa, the divination corpus, verses (*odu*) that linked the suppliant to parallel histories and/or related afflictions of former suppliants—legendary personages, now ancestral figures, and past sages and divinities. The therapeutic value of this was to ally the suppliant, psychically, to forces within the entirety of her healing culture—including the history of her own people. Sometimes this exercise in invocation would be continued by the suppliant in her own home, as accompaniment to the medication and prescribed sacrifices. Only then did I understand why the babalawo coached some suppliants until they had the few incantatory lines word-perfect. It was essential to the efficacy of the prescription, the sacrifice, or daily procedure. The post-visitation exercise could vary from bathing in a stream to visiting an ancestral shrine or historic spot. The incantations invoked the innate properties of the medication, augmented their potency, and brought the gods and ancestors who had passed through similar travails into partnership in the healing process.

This then is the binding network of mortals, deities, and nature that Christians and Moslems pronounced "pagan," "infidel," "demonic," etc., and moved to proscribe and destroy on the African continent, substituting, often through violence, their own faiths, which are based no less on structures of superstition though are perhaps more elegant, architecturally imposing, or seductively packaged. At the heart of it all, however, is nothing more than an article of faith sustained by dogmatism.

Poetry in liturgy is common to most religions, perhaps the most powerful element, far more powerful than any alleged intrinsic truths of the religions themselves. Poetry, or, sometimes, sheer lyricism and mesmerizing rhetoric, these are tools that are natural to or cultivated by charismatic leaders in any culture, irrespective of the purpose to which such attributes are turned, secular or religious. The poetic repertory of African religious invocations—with or without the invocation of the names of deities—is additionally reflected today in those commonplace proverbs, social lyrics, and epic renditions that provide the richness of much of traditional literature, as well as the musicality of some languages. Here, as example, is one of my favorites, a favorite perhaps on account of my itinerant destiny, but one that exquisitely summarizes much of the foregoing, the interweaving of protective invocation with a summons to—in this case—the mere alliterative potency of the words:

Mo ja'we igbegbe
Ki won ma gbagbe mi

Mo ja'we oni tete

Ki won ma te mi m'ole

I plucked the leaves of gbegbe/Lest I be forgotten/I plucked the leaves of tete/Lest I be trodden under.[1]

A brief exposition, again to convey the complex logic that goes into this process of fortification in which the forces of the unseen, operating through Nature, are invoked: that which can injure me is now turned into a captive, or an ally. It does appear that we cannot escape the domination of the homeopathic, after all!

However, Orunmila, god of divination and wisdom, would sagely nod approval, and Orisa-oko, presiding deity of the vegetative world, would give his blessing to the voyaging suppliant. They would also dart a mocking smile in the direction of the closed minds of other religions, the "world religions," among them those who press wafers to the lips of

1. This is one of those familiar instances of a pure play on the sound of words. It builds on the fact that the Yoruba, like a number of African languages, is tonal, and while the same syllable may transmit many meanings, depending on the tone, so may a uni-tonal syllable provide, depending on its context, more than one meaning. The origin of that song would be traceable, I am certain, to prayers for the well-being of a voyager who has consulted the priest for fortifications against the perils of the journey, and also seeks to placate his anxieties lest he fade out of the memories and concerns of those he leaves behind. The undesired properties of the leaf "gbegbe," and the vegetable "tete"—negative properties only by sound association—are deliberately evoked, then exorcised. "Gbagbe"—close in sound to "gbegbe," the leaf, means to forget. By plucking and possessing the leaves of gbegbe a contrary empathy is invoked, and the voyager ensures that his fate shall not be found in gbagbe—to be forgotten. Similarly "te," which means "to step upon," "to oppress," is accorded a contrary indication. I pluck and guard the tete leaves, thereby ensuring that I control the negative potential in its constitutive phoneme—"te."

their followers to ingest the body of their sainted god, or their rivals in world status who race round a designated slab of rock and cast stones at it to ward off the devil, year after year. Yes, even at those who, centuries after the Age of Reason and its underlying spirit of enquiry, still deem a continent backward and satanic that had proved itself capable of weaving and sustaining such a rich tapestry of intuitive forces. But then, did they know of, or seriously penetrate, such systems of belief? No, their sources remained missionary missives. Despite them all, however, Africa survives to teach the world—even without proselytizing.

One acknowledges, without equivocation, the progress that has been made in medicine through scientific research, the World Health Organization, and other bodies in the eradication of diseases, so we can only urge that the foregoing is not misunderstood. My family remains proud of the fact that a member of our extended branches served, long before the now routine recognition of African expertise, as the deputy director-general of the World Health Organization in Geneva. He also was the first African to institutionalize the traditional approach to psychiatric medicine—in the same Abeokuta where this inquisitive child watched the babalawo at work on both psychiatric and physiological disorders. Yet another member—one of the most empathetic beings in the world—nevertheless began his career as minister of health with the casual, condescending dismissal of any virtue in traditional medicine—they were all charlatans or, at best, unscientific. Before a year in office, however, having come face to face with hitherto unknown—to him—areas of verifiable efficacy, he became a cautious convert to the untapped potential of traditional medicine.

Our interest here is simply to relate the science of healing to the holism of faiths, of which a most potent aspect is the *Word,* the lyricism and poetry of healing which acts both therapeutically and homeopathically. When I proffer the following—just one more—sample, for instance, I do not intend for a moment to belittle the work done by the Jimmy Carter Foundation in the eradication of the guinea-worm scourge in West Africa—the Yoruba world would disown me, for a start, found guilty of the crime of exclusionism! It only happens to be a convenient example of the marriage of herbal treatment with the incantatory, one that I found among my father's papers. It had been sent to him by his father, when the family was plagued by that ailment, almost on a recurrent basis. We all know today that prevention, at the stage of drinking water or wading in stagnant pools, is the surest answer to the guinea worm. At that time, however, the actual entry points for these tormentors were something of a mystery.

No matter, certain members of the household appeared to be chronic victims of that condition, as my grandfather discovered after a number of visits to our home in Abeokuta. He returned to Isara, consulted his traditional healer, then sent a courier with the necessary items—there were herbs, barks for grinding, some mineral powder, etc., all to be dissolved in fermented corn juice or whatever else—I forget now. Fortunately, the main instructions were on a sheet of paper, as were the lines meant to be recited each morning to encourage the worm to emerge from the body, where it would be wound up gradually and prevented from retreating deeper into the flesh. It is difficult to imagine these days, but this was the procedure for expelling the guinea worm from the foot—gradually, but effectively. I still recall a few lines from that lyric:

> Oteere inu, oteere ode
> Onibode awo ara, opaara l'agbara eje
> A o le ni k'omo onle ma wole
> A o le ni ki baale ma t'ele
> Sugbon bi a f'alejo si ni ngbe
> Ibi a t'eni si l'alarinjo nfehin l'ole
> Onibode ara, ya a ma teri b'ode
> Amookun odo, ya a ma y'ori b'ode. . . .

Roughly—and it can only be very roughly indeed when translated into a language that lacks the tonal pyrotechnics of the Yoruba language—it goes thus:

> You that slither in the interior/you that slither on the out-
> side/Gatekeeper of the skin/wanderer within the blood ves-
> sels/We cannot say tell the child of the house not to enter/
> We cannot tell the Elder of the land not to tread earth/
> But it is where we place the guest that he lodges/It is where
> we spread the voyager's mat that he reposes/Gatekeeper of
> the skin, let us see your head beyond the porch/Diver in the
> deeps, break surface with your head. . . .

These are claimed potencies much derided or dismissed by the western-educated mind, but it is from within such resources that not only the religion but the full richness of Africa's literary wealth—oral, ancient and contemporary, of the continent and the Diaspora, written and rhetorical—can best be appreciated. A product originally of such traditions but now a Christian, born-again and church elder, a member of the Eminent Persons Group who visited Nelson Mandela while he was still trapped on Robben Island, a former head of state, smarting afterward from shared humiliation after his visit to Robben Island, forgot his statesman status and Christian avocation and reverted to his traditional repertory as he unleashed a *cri de coeur* in words that went: "Where is our *egbe*? Where is our *onde*? Where is our famed *juju* to take out these perpetrators of hideous injustice on our own soil?"

Words to that effect, and though eventually a disgraced, proven hypocritical ruler in his own country of Nigeria, rendering suspect even his passionate utterances at the time as being nothing more than a politician's attention-grabbing flam, they were nevertheless words that struck a chord in the traditional armory of most Africans. For it is not merely the beneficent gods and their potencies, their curative and fortifying interventions that occupy the African pantheons, but also the combative, even malevolent, who can be invoked to work against the enemy. Of course, such an aspect of their functions—depending on circumstances—may be regarded as preventive, or defensive assault. Effective or not, they are part of the secrets of the African continent, no less improbable than the bending of forks through sheer willpower, as advocated by the "para-psychic" Uri Geller, or the reliance of one American president at least—and his wife—on American witchdoctors, otherwise known as crystal-gazers. One can only open up a little window at a time on that rambling edifice of mystery rooms known as the African continent—it will be decades yet, if not centuries, before she yields up all her secrets, and much of it, alas, will end up in the least sympathetic—but most enterprising—hands. Sufficient for us is the creative use to which such mysteries are put, enabling, at the very least, the recovery of the bitter-sweet nostalgia of time past but not lost, such as Camara Laye's lyrical evocation of childhood in the classic work *The Dark Child.*

No, insufficiently celebrated remains the fate of this continuity between such traditional resources and contemporary creative minds, so perhaps a few pointers should come in here, usefully. If I had to select a single work that captures the accessible mystery of African spiritual-ity, its fussless integration into the mundane processes of productive existence, it would be this. Perhaps it has to do with the fact that the unnamed deity presiding in Laye's work is my own adopted demiurge, Ogun, the god of metallurgy (and thus the protector of blacksmiths, engineers, etc., the lyric, creativity, and war!). Personal empathy apart, however, *The Dark Child* remains one of the continent's most masterful evocations of a vanishing childhood idyll. It is dominated by the portrai-ture of the author's father, a blacksmith, through whose animistic dis-course and rituals Camara Laye ink-washes into life a background of the forge with images that fuse the world of metallurgy and craft with the pharmacopia of the healer. The solvent, as usual in works of this nature, is the lyricism of incantatory, often haunting language, a solvent that dissolves even the family totem, a snake, into spiritual membership of the household, integrated into family history and activities, unharmed and harmless, slithering in and out at a tranquil pace that reflects the very rhythm of household existence. A visitor to Ouidah, in the Repub-lic of Benin, and the Shrine of Pythons will recognize, without much effort, that inner harmony of man and the creatures of his natural environment that remains the elusive quest of contemporary man.

Across the Atlantic in the Diaspora, the traditional healer, still armed with the wisdom of the mother continent, remained equally active and is celebrated in the literature of dispersal. Daniel Maximin of Guadeloupe created one such figure in the person of Mother Bea—mystical yet efficacious and down to earth. The pharmaceutical knowledge that had been handed down to her from her ancestors enables her not only to heal but, where necessary, to kill her oppressors. Her reincarnated personalities dominate the struggle of the slaves for their liberation, efficacious both in her auguries and psychic estimations as in her down-to-earth, practical knowledge of herbs, a knowledge that she puts to revolutionary use when she extracts the necessary poisons to eliminate her tormentors.

Tituba, a Maryse Conde creation—Conde is a compatriot of Daniel Maximin—is another exemplar in the same mode, derided but much sought after following the failure of western medicine in the treatment of her slavemasters. A careful reading of Arthur Miller's *The Crucible* reveals that his portrayal of the African slave woman at the center of the witch hysteria is credited with genuine diagnostic intelligence and the corresponding herbal knowledge, recognized as such by some of the settlers of Salem but denounced as witchcraft by those whom the dramatist is careful to depict as ignorant, jaundiced, and bigoted. As sociological material, much of these sometimes fictionalized characters actually authenticate the curative armory that acccompanied the slaves into the Americas. Presiding over the day-to-day conversion of nature's forces are the deities, watchful, participating, never remote from their followers, the poetry of their liturgy indispensable for the pursuits of mortal followers in every field.

It is, not surprisingly, in psychiatric medicine especially that traditional healing has much to offer to the western world. In so many instances, western and, in particular, American psychiatry seems tailored to an existence of dependency and insecurity, to such a negative effect that one sometimes feels that the recuperation of the American psyche will begin only when the bulk of Freudian and Jungian texts are tossed into the nearest sea, the industry of annotation and revisionism of psychiatric theories criminalized, and a censorship law passed against the words "I am going to see my shrink," uttered with the same nonchalance as "I am going window-shopping" or "It's time for my gym session." Much of this authoritative/dependency relationship between psychiatrist and "patient" has addled the brains of much of American and European society—the younger generation especially—and twisted its collective psyche. Alas, it is now penetrating through to the African-American, especially of a middle-class mental orientation. African psychiatrists have begun to recognize the danger and are collaborating with traditional mental healers, refining their methods where needed but basing their procedures on the verifiable successes of ancient healers.

Then there are the traditional bone-setters found throughout the continent. Today, they receive patients referred to them routinely by western orthopaedic hospitals. Cases of startling recovery are recorded—to be distinguished from the soap opera of Christian faith healing that has become compulsive television viewing for addicts of the miraculous or of simply atrocious theater. This latter phenomenon, however, ironically reinforces the unintended. Spurious though a number of these "miracle" healings are, and sometimes spectacularly exposed as such, they also feed on that combination of spirituality and psychology—the foundation on which the foregoing has been posited. Rehearsed, often crudely performed, they profit from that ancient, traditional integration of the potency of supernatural invocation with the universe of the body.

But we can leave the invisible or mysterious out of the equation, there being so much lucrative commerce in charlatanism. Those who seek to unlock the forces of nature for the benefit of human well-being need not travel along psychic waves but along the dirt road to obscure but increasingly known villages where such knowledge is guarded and practicalized. Even within the urban domain, the health pages of Africa's media are, in any case, inundated daily with contributions by western-trained doctors and dieticians constantly at work investigating and disseminating the ways and findings—and the material sources!—of traditional healers, their millennia-old cures and preventive regimen for a variety of diseases whose names entered into western medical textbooks only within the past half century. Years of clinical work in the comparative and specific virtues of both schools have taught an increasing number of western-trained doctors humility, and expanded their universe of curative knowledge. Here is a specific (and likely to prove groundbreaking!) instance.

An African shrub, used by traditional healers since ancient times, has been the subject of clinical tests, going on for over seven years, that now appear to position it as a front runner for the cure of diabetes and a number of skin diseases, including skin cancer. A famous French cosmetic firm began to fund the research—by U.S.-based Nigerian medical researchers—quite early on and has now bought into the company set up for its commercial exploitation.

I cannot, however, conclude this exploration without a personal testimony of the most dramatic instance of the preservation and ongoing application of such "invisible" knowledge. This saga began for me in Los Angeles, to terminate in a clinic outside Accra, Ghana, a healing center whose reputation is becoming increasingly acknowledged, headed today by a Ghanaian doctor trained in the western tradition. The successes of that clinic on spinal injuries where the most famous specialized hospitals—such as Cedars-Sinai in Los Angeles—had failed, are fast becoming legendary. The patient in this instance was a relation by marriage, a young seaman domiciled near my exile home, and a naturalized American of Ghanaian origin. Jacob suffered a horrendous spinal injury while offloading containers on his ship. The accident took place off the Canadian coast, and thus he was first airlifted to a hospital in Seattle. Later, as his condition worsened, he was flown to Los Angeles to continue treatment.

Jacob T.'s agony was not a sight for weak stomachs. He considered suicide a few times, once, in sheer desperation, steering his wheelchair onto the street in the hope of being struck by traffic. It was at a much later stage that he was diagnosed as suffering from a particular form of spinal injury that was identified only in World War I, casually dismissed at the time as malingering. Several soldiers had been shot on this account, only to be posthumously rehabilitated. His employer, the shipping company, had a similar notion. T, they thought, was faking his agony, with an eye on litigation and damages. I have encountered victims of torture in my career, and when I looked into the clouded depths of Jacob's eyes, my immediate comment was that this man has undergone some truly bestial form of torture!

He underwent several surgical procedures. At one stage he was on nineteen different pills each day. A special device was inserted into his spine, and he was taught to adjust it through dosages of medication whenever the agony became intolerable. Later he was transferred to a special clinic where he stayed for six weeks in two separate sessions, mastering the life sentence art of pain management. It was only on account of the death of his mother during this period—a mother he had not seen since departure from Ghana twenty years earlier—that he undertook the immense risk of traveling to Ghana to wind up his family affairs. It was a lucky move, for it was on that visit that someone suggested this clinic that was founded and run on traditional medical practice. Skeptically, he tried it.

At the clinic his condition was immediately recognized, he reported. He was made to bring out all his medication. The doctor tossed them one by one into the rubbish bin, allowing him to keep only one but warning that he would be weaned off even that within a week. Then followed a process that was based on the application of a poultice made from local herbal leaves. The harvesting of those leaves, I later discovered, was an elaborate affair, a ritual scrupulously retained by the western-trained Ghanaian head of the institute. It is the one secret—the location of one of the component leaves for the making of the poultice—that is jealously guarded by the clinic. In the video documentary of the treatment procedure, cameras were stopped at the point where the harvesting procession was swallowed by the forest, to reemerge before dusk, bearing the precious foliage. The season, the time of day, the procession into the forest, the solemn chants and incantations—all are scrupulously observed, as they had been from a time no one can precisely recall.

Treatment began in June 2005, three years after his accident, three years of intense stretches of pain and chemically induced patches of relief. Exercises, carefully graduated, nearly unbearable pain at the beginning, then slow walks—his walking stick had been confiscated at the start of treatment—increasing to brisk, then supervised trotting around the compound's perimeter, to increased speed and distances. Special diet to boost the effect of medication—Jacob spent four to five weeks undergoing this treatment.

I was busy in my study in Upland when Jacob T. returned from Accra some weeks later. There was a knock on the door and I barked my irritated "Come in!" A man I failed to recognize entered, grinning. As I continued to stare, he broke into a Ghanaian dance—the *kpalongo!* Jacob? Jacob T.? Jacob, who, for three years, had been wheelchair bound, could just manage to limp from wheelchair to his permanent chair in the living room for his silent meditation with the television screen, and next to bed, always with a sturdy walking stick? It was with difficulty that I held back the tears.

The Yoruba logos, *Ase,* in its variants among African belief systems, unites Nature, as both nurturer and healer, with the human psyche for the body's and community's well-being. Thus it is appropriate to wind up this section with a verse of *Ase,* a word that is so difficult to translate out of the Yoruba language but perhaps is best rendered as the vital or animating pronouncement—one that invokes the full authority of whichever is the presiding Orisa at an event, the cosmos, and the forces and energies that are represented in Nature:

Aase, ko ni s'aise; Nitori awise ni t'Ifa,

Afose ni t'Orunmila

Ase egunmo nii se l'awujo efo

Ase ijimere nii se l'awujo eranko

Terekese naa nii se l'awujo owu

Gbogbo igi ti legbede ba f'owo ba nii dun

Ko se, k'o se ni t'ilakose

Yee a ba wi han ogbo ni ogbo i gbo

Yee a ba wi han igba ni igba i gba

Oro okete ba le so ni ile i gbo

A ba alagemo ba da l'Orisa i gba

Aro oun abuke ki i p'ohun Orisa da

Sango ki i ko ohun orogbo

Orisa ki i ko ohun obi

Obatala ki i ko ohun seseefun

So shall it be, it shall not fail to be/For fulfilment of the word is Ifa/Fulfilment of the voice is Orunmila/Egunmo holds sway at the harvest of vegetables/The baboon holds sway at the gathering of the beasts of the forest/The frosted cotton holds sway at the gathering place of cotton/All trees resound at the mere touch of the orang-outang/So shall it be, that it shall be is the portion of the river mussel/It is what we whisper to the keen-edged grass to which the grass listens/It is what we say to the tapper's cradle that the cradle receives/What the bush rodent tells the earth is what the earth undoubtedly hears/The mutations of the chameleon find approval among the deities/The lame and the hunchbacks do not neglect the voice of the deities/Sango never rejects the bitter ritual nut/No deity ever rejects the voice of the kola nut/Obatala will never reject the voice of the white coral bead. *A-a-se.* So shall it be.

7. The Spirituality of a Continent

FROM BODY TO SOUL, FROM THE physiological and mental ministrations we move closer to the spiritual ministry. Even within what should be a generous canopy of history, Africa has been cynically short-changed, and this is a negative reflection more on the outside world than on Africa herself, since what we observe within such judgmental societies is often at loggerheads with the claims of their own "civilizing mission" and leadership assumptions in matters of development. Beyond material development there is of course spiritual development, to which the worlds of Islam and Christianity especially lay preeminent claims, if not indeed claims of outright superiority. As with materiality, spirituality may elevate and ennoble, degrade and debase. The undiscovered—or neglected, indeed, despised—terrain of Africa's spirituality, which may hold answers to some of the material problems of the world is, as already stated, perhaps the most notorious of the many historic denials.

Religion—or, more accurately, fanaticism—has once again, and in such rabid form, bared its fangs in parts of the continent, turning Africa into a warring ground that has even thrown into disarray what are known as traditional alliances, while rendering impotent the umbrella organization that is sworn to uphold the constitutional will of the African peoples. It is not sufficient therefore to merely outline the realities within the spiritual vacuum that Africa was considered to be before the entry of the two "world" religions, but also some significant, mostly contrasting properties of the intruders. After all, the battle for the "soul" of Africa, a battle that is being waged by violent conscription, began elsewhere but will likely conclude on the continent. If Africa falls to the will of the fanatic, then the insecurity of the world should be accepted as its future and permanent condition. There are no other options.

In what forms did that continent express its spirituality before the advent of Islam and Christianity? The answer is easiest grasped in the negative—and that answer is: not in any violent or conscriptive form. Unlike in other parts of the globe, religion on the continent has always been a process of relating to phenomena that surround man—including unseen forces—primarily in a personal way, but collectively also in rites of notation, celebration, and consolidation of the community. The most famous of these systems is accepted by many to be that of the Yoruba people of the Western Coast of Nigeria, and can be safely elected as the paradigm of spirituality for virtually every corner of the continent— whether such religions are described as fetishism, animism, ancestor worship, voodoo, or spirit worship—but not where they are facilely conflated with cults. Cults are mostly secretive instruments of power, even where they can be proved to have sprung from the genuine religion. Each and every one of Africa's religions is animated through negotiations— including symbolic—by the human entity with the forces that surround it, and the need to invoke, placate, or co-opt the forces of nature for the survival of his species.

One of the most astonishing claims for monotheism is the baseless notion that it represents the pinnacle of religious consciousness of which man is capable. That such a claim should be supported by any product of African society—for example, Bolaji Idowu's *Olodumare: God in Yoruba Belief*—is not unexpected, since such scholars are converts to Christian theology anyway. Where one is compelled to take issue is with those who claim to speak as philosophers or social scientists, those who, like Hegel, go even further to state that a major defect in the African's intelligence is his incapacity to conceive of a unified godhead. Such claims are, first of all, sheer falsities, since religions such as the Orisa actually acknowledge the existence of a supreme deity. Next, there is absolutely no foundation in reason or logic that the ascending order of godhead in monotheistic form represents a higher development in man's conceptual capacities than the obverse. It is no more valid than an opinion that favors despotism above democracy. Religion, alas, on the African continent, has moved in recent times beyond the luxury of mere abstraction or academic exercise. It has leapt to the forefront of global concern, where its claims are promoted not by mystic incantations and the intuitions of ruminant clerics but by the latest in the technology of mass destruction, randomly unleashed for the maximum exaction on innocent humanity. It threatens the very fabric of a continent that, only a decade or so ago, considered herself immune from the lunacy of faiths, a landmass that is barely recovering from centuries of physical wreckage. Never, for instance, until this decade, would one have encountered, in a Nigerian op-ed headline, the anguished cry KILLING IS BELIEVING?

All religions are unique in some way—if they were not, there would be no religious conflicts, so perhaps this is one of those instances where variety is not so much the spice of life as the trigger of strife. Yet all religions aspire toward the same nebulous destination—union with, or intimation of, the presence of godhead in present existence or in afterlife. The instinct toward disruption of individual or collective voyages toward this destination should therefore be considered a malformation in human understanding, or a conscious pursuit of a totally disconnected agenda from that of religious fulfillment. That instinct, without question, has its foundation in Power.

Africa is filled with religions that point the way to the harmonization of faiths; it is the loss of the world that many of them are little known, their unassuming, ancient wisdoms being superstructurally dwarfed by the admittedly often awe-inspiring monuments on the world's landscape—cathedrals, mosques, temples, and shrines—and indeed by the challenging paradoxes of their exegeses. I say paradoxes because they are no more than intellectual constructs on foundations of the unproven and unprovable. The disquisitions—just to take one single but mesmerizing aspect of Christian theology—on transubstantiation alone from the most ancient manuscripts will fill the shelves of a cavernous university library from floor to ceiling. Yet these all-consuming debates and formal encyclicals are constructed on what we may term a proliferating autogeny within a hermetic realm—what is at the core of arguments need not be true; it is sufficient that the layers upon layers of dialectical constructs fit snugly on top of one another. There need not be any substance at the core, any more than in an onion. And when one examines the ancient manuscripts, the lovingly illuminated manuscripts especially of the so-called Dark and Middle Ages, when those artistic-minded monks of supreme devotion had nothing else to do during the long dark nights of winter seasons, and had only saints, angels, and demons as outlets for expressing their love for and injunctions to humanity, those manuscripts inspire awe and admiration in us today, and of course reinforce the beliefs of multitudes. So do the Sanskrits, the Hindu Veda, the prayer scrolls in Buddhist temples, or the ancient texts of the Holy Koran.

Those very seductions that are the outward embellishments of religions are also recognizable as competitive attributes of the secular world, especially those that are raised to ideological ascendancies. The monumental achievements of either fascism or communism, the choreographed splendor and pageantry that trumpeted their existence, the arts, architecture, and ideological treatises still impress or repel us. Their aesthetic virtues may not amount to much—witness the architectural horrors of the Third Reich or East European communist regimes—but the sheer grandiose scale of their conception and execution continue to astound, even though neither ideology has presented the world with any lasting truths. Even thus must we learn to view the existence of cathedrals and mosques, of temples and shrines, as we feast our eyes on their illuminated scriptures, are enraptured by their spiritually elevating music, and succumb to the mystery of their rituals. Not one of these, or any religion known to humanity, can affirm in any testable way the eternal verities of whatever "truths" they espouse.

By contrast, apart from its own philosophical literature, and apart from that short-lived bemusing experimentation from the French

Revolution—the Festival of Reason—humanism, for its part, has no ostentatious monuments or rituals that testify to any ineradicable virtues. Its monuments exist, of course; they are visible everywhere in the advances of civilization, in the arts and sciences, in the mundane handiwork of man and the constant enhancement of his productive capability and environment, but these are never labeled as such. The great symphonies, the classic sculptures from the Yoruba to the Arawaks, the successful orbiters and the failed Mars Lander are the monuments to humanism, though they are never mounted on a plinth labeled "Humanism." So, paradoxically but vibrantly, are "invisible religions" such as Orisa, the invisible order of the secular gods. But despite the absence of such nominal appropriation, we find that humanism does enjoy, at the very least, some element of lip service paid to its tenets by all religions. Indeed, these religions appear to fall over one another in attempting to ground their concerns in the elevation of humankind, just as the failed, contending ideologies attempted to root their principles in the primacy of humane values—egalitarianism, end of exploitation, universal brotherhood, etc., etc. What we must pursue, therefore, is not a competitive, bruising arena for the claims of ideology or religion but an open marketplace of both ideas and faiths. It is within this context, without any ambiguity, that the Orisa and their body of divine precepts, Ifa, prove of great humanistic value in the realm of religion. As quest, as the principle of spiritual enquiry, Ifa exemplifies this field of accommodation for all seekers, under no matter what structure of belief.

This ancient religion that we have co-opted as a guide into our exploration of a noninterfering order of faith and spirituality proposes

that "warfare" between religions need not be. Its very nature protects it
from the bellicose instinct that leads followers of other beliefs to defend
even the most trivial annotation of their doctrinal text with their lives
or, more accurately, with the lives of others, conveniently designated
infidels, unbelievers, apostates, enemies of God, and other charitable
epithets. We shall let this religion demonstrate that perhaps, since religion is so evidently entrenched in the human psyche, humanity is better
served by the adoption of secularized deities than by those other gods
of undoubtedly entrancing liturgies that are evoked as control zones on
humanity, tyrannized over by mortals, no different from ourselves.

But—secular deities? What an oxymoron! We shall examine that
notion as we proceed. The essential virtue that is attributable to our exemplar, the Orisa religion, practiced by a people known as the Yoruba,
indigenes of the West Coast of Africa—that special virtue is found in
the reduced status of priesthood in its accustomed intermediary role.
This role, in many other religions, tends to sanctify the priesthood as
a class apart and encourages a monopoly of access to the experience of
godhead, turning priests into privileged, often dictatorial recipients and
custodians of Revelation. From that spiritual function it is only a short
step to secular control—habits, tastes, even personal relationships—indeed, all aspects of secular life which properly belongs to other structures
of society, including its politics. That is the problem. After millennia of
recorded human history it becomes easy enough to accept that religion,
or experiences that come to be grouped under that name, may have been
preprogrammed into the human genome, so it is in our own interest to
explore those religious brands which, for one reason or the other, either

have never habored the violent strain of dogmatic interventions in social life or have somehow evolved away from such suprahuman tendencies.

There are of course several of these conveniently termed invisible religions, since they are overshadowed, to the point of near invisibility by other elaborate, over endowed, over annotated, and territorially rapacious designated world religions. Prominent among these "invisible" moral challengers is the Orisa, one whose attributes are such that one can claim with absolute confidence that it could never have produced the Roman Catholic Inquisition. The notion of a Crusade or a Jihad as historically and presently understood and pursued is inconceivable in this faith. Such considerations, in addition to its history of involuntary expansion—quite unlike the expansionist history of others based on conquest, enforced conversion, iconoclasm, and war—offer up this singular religion as a potential model for the spiritual cravings of seekers who might wonder why the inherent sublimity of so many spiritual structures of the world—most notoriously the two claimants to primacy—Judeo-Christianity and Islam—are soaked in intolerance, blood, hatred, and insecurity, evincing every form of antihumanist deadliness as basic conditions for their very survival.

The prediction of the African-American sociologist W. E. B. Du Bois that the preeminent issue of the twentieth century would be that of race has given way to the crisis of religion in the twenty-first. One is tempted to advance this even further, to phrase it in near apocalyptic terms: given the surge of the fanatical temper that consistently threatens to consume the world, both from ancient and in contemporary times, involving the denial of the human primacy in secular designs, one wonders if the question for our times should not be: Can religion peacefully cohabit with humanism in the twenty-first? In certain parts of the world the question indeed appears to be: Can religion cohabit with humanity itself? Such is the degree to which religion has either been central to, or has facilitated, the deadliness of conflicts, prodigally sacrificing humanity on altars erected even to mere differences in doctrinal niceties or historical interpretations, and most lethally when this occurs within the same faith.

Let us, however, confine ourselves within the former, more manageable terrain, one that covers the widening claims of religion over secular prerogatives, and permit ourselves merely to speculate whether the religious impulse and the humanist pursuit were ever intended to occupy any zone of mutual accommodation. Fifty years ago—let us say around the middle of the twentieth century, such a question would not have leapt to mind. It is not that no events of a decidedly antihumanist determination ever shook our world to its very foundations, it is simply that we find ourselves in a time of global fissures in which religion is playing an increasingly conspicuous role, a role that one hoped had disappeared with the European Dark Ages, even if we chose to leapfrog the intervening centuries into that age from perhaps the earliest recorded martyrdom in the territorial contest between the secular and the religious—the execution of Socrates by hemlock for his religious—more accurately, irreligious—convictions. In varying potencies and methods of application, that cup of hemlock seems to have remained suspended over protagonists on either side of the theocratic and secular divide, the former mostly administering. That cup has been passed on to the African continent, which finds itself convulsing on the unaccustomed communion.

It is, however, useful to place the depredations wrought by religion in context. The antireligious agenda is not necessarily in alliance with, or pursuing, the same goals as secularism or its close ally, humanism, even as assaults on the religious order do not necessarily espouse the cause of secular humanism. Responsibility for some of the most infamous crimes against humanity in the twentieth century could hardly be blamed on religion. The pernicious Nazi world-view that produced the Holocaust at least had the sense of restraint—or simply self-confidence—not to justify its crimes under the banner of any religion. At the opposite end of the ideological polarity, Josef Stalin, who rivaled Adolf Hitler in the magnitude of human decimation, stuck religiously—more accurately, nonreligiously—to the vision (not divine revelation) of a classless society, in the promotion of which he persecuted all religions, sealed up places of worship as fervently as he eliminated millions of so-called *kulaks,* ideological revisionists and deviationists, including some of the finest scientists and humanists of that nation. Stalin has been followed since by disciples on various levels of humanophobia—Pol Pot of Cambodia, Miriam Mengistu of Ethiopia, etc.—who have done their best to rival and exceed the worst excesses of Hitler or Stalin, speaking in comparative terms of populations under their control.

For some of these world-infamous antihumanists, it is reasonable to propose that ideology was a mere substitute for religion, which is one reason why one entertains a suspicion that the religious impulse may actually have been inserted into the human genome from a very early stage of human evolution. Nomenclatures differ. One may claim for itself a scientifically deduced conclusion to the history of humanity, enshrined in profuse texts of dubious certitudes, while the other proceeds along the path of Revelation, sanctified by its inviolate scriptures. The trite commentary, however, is that the Marxist vision of scientific social transformation, even if that society was turned into a virtual necropolis, was not much different from the religious revelationism of the Taliban. The Hutu genocidaires who butchered over three-quarters of a million people in the record time of some ten to twelve days were proponents of a purism of a distinctly religious fervor, propelled by a sense of pre-destination and infallibility, not much different from the destination of the South African Boers—a Nazified vision of race supremacy and purity. Neither of these claimed to be inspired by religion as primary cause, although of course the authority of the Bible was invoked, and the Lutheran church co-opted into affirmations of the Apartheid doctrine of race supremacy. It is important to recall also that some of the leaders of the Rwandan massacre were Christian priests who enthusiastically deployed their religious status in the promotion of that crime. Several of them, as often attested in the International Court for Crimes against Humanity in Arusha, Tanzania, actually lured their victims into churches, guaranteeing them sanctuary, then summoned the Hutu killer squads, the *interehamwe*, and the military, to commence their gory task. Decidedly religion—or more accurately, the Church—was implicated but, religion was never argued as the basis of this call to the banalization of humanity.

Now that we have taken care to pay dues to such exceptions, we may safely claim that several centuries after the Crusades, the Inquisition, the Jihad, and their enthusiastic pogroms of infidels and heretics of the world, the promulgation of a killing religious transcendentalism on a global scale—that is, religion as a killing device, guarantor of impunity and homicidal inspiration, is a recent phenomenon, and one that seems determined to sweep us all into the next world without notice, ostensibly to rescue us from eternal perdition.

With such a background, and given the knowledge of the proneness of religion—or simply its proponents—to homicidal outbreaks, be it only as a complicating factor in sociopolitical conflicts on a minor or major scale, of brief or prolonged duration, in places as culturally diverse as Nigeria, Ireland, India, the Soviet Union, Indonesia, etc., and with a fragmenting consistency in Somalia, such eruptions guaranteed to be an occurrence, an influence, and a factor somewhere across the globe, and at any given moment even in our so-called modern times, it would be understandable if religion were given short shrift in any exercise that seeks to weigh its positives against its negatives. The very latest of these eruptions, the sanguinary divisions in Somalia, nearly drives one to despair on behalf of the secular imperative.

Again we shall concede some enabling factors for the ascendancy of religious indoctrination—social and cultural dispositions, governmental neglect, state of insecurity that arises from the diminishing capacities of a failed state, and roaming armies of the unemployed, the marginalized, and socially dispossessed, etc.—these are all undeniable—but the geopolitics of religion is clearly at the root of even this most recent Somali conflict. In Somalia, unlike Sudan, where all the contestants are of one faith—Islam—it does not require the actual self-attribution of structures of the Somali insurgents, such as the so-called Islamic Courts Union, to recognize the religious component—indeed, imperative—of

that ongoing civil convulsion. The situation is further clarified by the religious partisanship of the government of Ethiopia, adherents of an ancient branch of Christianity, whose forces once flushed out the Islamists
from the seat of power in Mogadishu—at least temporarily. Mobiliza-
tion, organization, allegiance, and indeed fanatic dedication on one part
most obviously fueled the intensity of the carnage. For the foot soldiers,
this is not in question—they are virtual zombies of an impenetrable
religious seizure. Regarding the leadership, those seasoned manipulators
of the irrational sentiment of faith, power is the prize, as always, even
as a fundamentalist grounding of religious conviction ministers blindly
to power. Allowing for materialist complications here and there, including a sturdy impulsion to expel foreign elements from society, we find
ourselves firmly in the territory of religion as an assiduous handmaiden
to the territorial pursuit of power and the enthronement of fascism.
Between the doctrine of racial purity and that of ideological/spiritual
purity, let who will delineate the minutiae of daily consequences for
humanity.

Given the replication of these scenarios virtually everywhere, from
the Soviet Union—Chechnya—to Indonesia's Aceh islands and other places
outside the mainstream world observatory, religious advocacy of an increasingly antihumanist dimension makes one wish that religion would
simply go away, leaving humanity with other problems that the world
already possesses in superabundance. Let us, however, play the devil's
advocate for a little while—even the devil does have his uses, if only as a
metaphor of instruction.

We are faced with the danger of not knowing, of having to speculate over the possibility that religion may also be a restraining factor for even more reckless antihumanist drives, that the nonquantifiable, often invisible spiritual checks provided by religion itself may have placed an imperceptible lid on the cauldron of the world's existential crisis. That is the problem one encounters in attempting to assess the world accurately in the parlous condition in which it frequently finds itself. By this I mean that, paradoxically, the daunting picture that results from our assessment of the global situation may lead us to concede, at least theoretically, that our situation could be much worse without religion. Trying to determine what social factors—habits, beliefs, communication explosion, technology, or other preoccupations—may be holding off Armageddon, one may indeed arrive at the possibility, just the possibility, that the existence of religion, with its unfathomable influence on the human mind, may have been just as crucial to human survival— again, just as speculatively—as the arts of diplomacy, the elevating role of the arts, access to social facilities, reduction of poverty, the euphoria of pop concerts, soccer, American football or basketball, or the more tangible activities of peacekeeping organizations all over the world. In other words, religion may have contributed to the very continuance of existence, as it has certainly contributed to the stabilization of innumerable individual psyches.

Take the prisoner—the role of religion in prisons for the social rehabilitation of the inmate is not wholly negligible—our most famous example is perhaps Malcolm X, who converted to Islam. The poet, playwright, and irrepressible wit Oscar Wilde, despite his threnody, *The Ballad of Redding Gaol,* does not appear to have undergone any permanent transformation, but he did provide the world some moving lines of soul-searching in adversity. Not that it is recommended that one end up in prison in order to produce poetry of sublimity or solace—the world is not short of religious poets who have never seen the inside of a prison, both the contemplative, like Khalil Gibran, and the tortured, like Gerard Manley Hopkins.

Let us borrow an analogy from the medical sciences: even an accurately diagnosed disease does not preclude the potential of that very ailment in the prevention of worse afflictions. A timely migraine may, for all we know, have prevented a stroke. A mere two decades ago we learned that thalidomide, that scourge of pregnant mothers in the nineteen-fifties and sixties in its creation of infant deformities, is now being used to treat certain forms of cancer, with impressive results. In the field of human transformation, for some of us, it is only such considerations— apart from the impracticality—that pull us back from embarking on a campaign for anathemizing all the historic structures that religion has spawned. We would mobilize those famous—or infamous, depending on point of view—and ubiquitous U.S. "injury lawyers" to sue religion as a justiciable entity, institute a class action against it in the International Court at The Hague, have it condemned for crimes against humanity and deported on a one-way passage via the next shuttle flight into outer space.

The intensification of religious zealotry all over the world after the collapse of its main rival, though secular, ideology—communism—proves that nature does indeed abhor a vacuum, and if, miraculously, religion were to vanish magically—perhaps one should say, miraculously—as its final miracle on earth, an immeasurable gift of absence—who knows what else might take its place! American football? Videogames, perhaps? Reality shows? Wine tastings? Or maybe jogging? To sum up this part of our discourse, let us take consolation in viewing religion through the same paradoxical lens as one views the operations of homeopathy. Karl Marx was wrong—his famous dismissive statement was not totally accurate. Religion is not so much the opium of the people as it is the homeopathy of the human Condition.

Invading the world of one of these homeopathic structures—Orisa religion—requires that we try to redress certain opportunistic notions of what we actually designate religion. It is a necessary exercise, indeed part of the narrative of African spirituality, since it responds to the dismissive ploy of denigration that was so beloved by Christian missionaries in soon to be colonized regions of Africa and Asia. For these Bible warriors, African spiritual observances could not be counted as religions but as fetish worship, superstitions, heathenism, cultic or satanic manifestations. Aware of the existence of cults, usually as power devices that operated through secret rituals, oath-taking, and thus, fear of the vengeance of malevolent forces for apostates and oath-breakers, these were conveniently grouped together with religions, whereas they were, if anything, purely political instruments of power and terror. They were used to acquire wealth, consolidate political positions, and keep other sections of the community—most often the female sex—in their place, though we should bear in mind that in certain African societies women also operated through some powerful cults of their own, such as the famous *Iya mi* cult of former Dahomey—now Republic of Benin—or the *Gelede* of

Western Nigeria. Also, under foreign occupation, the rise of cultism is a common enough phenomenon, an adopted instrument of secrecy and solidarity in liberation struggles. Cults may attach to religion in order to harvest a ready membership and ride on spiritual intensity, but cults do not require a deity.

Religion is built on the evocation of deities; a religion without a god, or the celebrated essence of one, is simply not a religion. At the same time it is necessary to look out for cultists who invoke the name of a deity. One such, a claimant to Christianity, founded a most successful cult in Uganda. It resulted in an organized mass murder of his believers—Jamestown style, only by arson. And he did not partake of this terminal baptism by fire, having made good his escape with all his disciples' worldly goods. The early Christian evangelists did not even stoop to examine such differences: it was more convenient to bury religion under a sweeping cultic apprehension, thus conveniently demonize and/or dismiss the existence of the former.

Let us make special mention at this point of a pertinent example of such demonization—this time, in the literal sense. When the missionaries arrived in African societies to commence their task of conversion, they felt handicapped because, in many instances, they could not isolate the concept of the devil or of Satan. It must have been a serious setback, since only through the establishment of the notion of sin could these "heathens" be made aware of the peril in which their souls stood—unless they converted. Damnation and salvation—these were the axes of the cross on which the heathen soul must be stretched, then steered triumphantly toward the latter. To impress upon the desired convertites

their condition in sin, and thus as damned, the early Christian missionaries desperately needed the services of that obliging agent—the devil!
In the case of the Yoruba, they examined all potential candidates and
opted for Esu—spelled Exu in Brazil.

This was quite convenient, since Esu is the most ubiquitous of
all the deities, being their messenger, and a complex yet "mischievous"
one to boot. He sits at the crossroads and confuses the wisest of mortals
and gods. Such is his unpredictable nature that the Yoruba never build
a shrine to him within the home. Often represented in sculpture and
in narratives of his exploits as a Janus-face, his place is on the doorstep
and at the crossroads, where sacrifices are made to him to guarantee his
noninterference in human affairs or to secure his benevolent patronage.
Even during festivals of the principal deities, the first morsel is set aside
for Esu and, in commencing any ceremony, mortals consider it wise to
implore Esu to restrain his prankish temperament. Esu, however, is anything but evil—the notion is as absurd as to deem a high-spirited child
a product of the devil. This deity represents the random, unpredictable factor in both divine and mortal affairs. Esu is the dialectician of
reality, a cautionary spirit who teaches that reality has more facets than
one. Trust not to appearances—that is the lesson of Esu, a lesson often
imparted the hard way. The observant will notice that I have quietly ma-
nipulated Esu into being our first encounter as we irreverently approach
the realm of Yoruba deities!

A child is born. Quite early in its life the parents discern in this new
organism traces of personality, those rudimentary tendencies, mate-

rial preferences, etc., that will someday coalesce into what we designate character—*Iwa*. This newcomer is taken to the babalawo—the priest of divination, who adds his tutored observations to the signs that have already been remarked by parents and relations. Ifa, the divination corpus, is central to the world of the Orisa and thus the babalawo sometimes will take the child through the actual divination process. Mostly, however, it is his shrewd eyes, extensive experience, and honed intuition that decide for him—this, he observes, is a child of Osun, the god of the rivers, or of Sango, of lightning and thunder, or Obatala, the divinity of purity. It does not matter that neither parent is a follower of any such deity, or that no one in the household or in the history of the family has ever been an initiate of the god—the child, it is accepted, brings his or her own *ori*—destiny, portion—into the world. It is futile to attempt to change it or to impose one on him.

Yet even this allotment of the child's spiritual aura is not definitive, nor is it exclusive. Some other events in that child's formative passage— a series of incidents, a display of special talent, creative or leadership precocity, or indeed some further revelation of earlier hidden traits such as a tendency toward clairvoyance, or simply the child's habit of enigmatic utterances—may lead the babalawo to conclude that a different guardian deity is indicated for the child, or an additional one. And thus a new deity is admitted into the household. There is no friction, no hostility. All gods, the Yoruba understand, are manifestations of universal phenomena of which humanity is also a part. Ifa is replete with *odu*—those verses that form a compendium of morality tales, historic vignettes, and curative prescriptions—verses that narrate at the same time the experiences of both mortals and immortals for whom Ifa divined, counseled, and who either chose to obey or ignore Ifa. The skeptics are neither penalized nor hounded by any supernatural forces. The narratives indicate that they simply go their way.

A little time on the personality of, as well as the social/professional situating of the babalawo, or indeed of the priesthood of the deities, is essential, just to keep our feet firmly on the earth of reality, lest we incur the wrath of Ifa himself. Ifa does not tolerate false attributions, even as glamorization: the babalawo—or priest of Ifa—is mortal. The priesthood class often represents the negative side of intermediation with the deities—need we recall the predatory sexual perversions across the globe within the Roman Catholic priesthood, virtually institutionalized from the prolonged policy of concealment? Or the role of mullahs in the war of mutual attrition between Shiites and Sunnis, even where this involved violent repudiation of the ancient tradition of the sanctity of holy places and pilgrimages? Orisa priesthood confessedly cannot compete with such levels of criminal delinquency; nonetheless, we must not shy away from their place within the universal deficit, so here is one sobering instance, lodged in tradition. The priests of Sango, historically, were not above profiting from human disaster and attributing lightning strikes to the ire of the god who singled out malefactors for punishment. The entire possessions of such unfortunates, sometimes including even those of their relations lodged in the same household, were instantly seized by such priests of Sango.

And yet the babalawo, in his unsullied state of a divine functionaire, represents the noblest, most self-denying virtues in the entire world of the Orisa. Embedded in his training is a rejection of profit—probe any true babalawo and he confesses that he dare not ply his calling for profit, or the gods will deprive him of his divination skills. The sentence is final. The babalawo is thus the personification of the virtues of self-denial, abstemiousness, and even penury.

The calling has not escaped corruption, especially in modern times. Some prominent babalawo now indulge in the once unthinkable—charge fees, exhorbitant ones at that, of their clients. They now boast of what, in Nigeria, we call "rosy cheeks." Academics, having earned their spurs through dissertations on Ifa, have become notorious for "initiating" spiritual seekers in the Caribbean and Brazil into the divination fold—the going rate was $5,000 per head—for a spurious ceremony larded with a jumbled invocation of a verse or two from Ifa, with presentation of a certificate to be hung on the wall of their living room as a diploma. These are the latter-day descendants of the vulturine branch of Sango priests. Such abomination was rare even into the sixties and seventies of the last century. Outsiders turned citizens of the Orisa world, such as the Austrian-German Ulli Beier and his wife, Susan Wenger, who have delved deeply into Orisa communities, have testified to the lived oaths of penury and abstemiousness that characterized the true servitors of Ifa. My intimate interactions with this endangered species sometimes evoked parallels with rare political leaders of the Julius Nyerere mold, a leader who died possessed of no more than a modest cottage and his annual pension. Such is the rarity of exemplars of the ethos of the babalawo on the African scene, increasingly hard to find.

Still, nowhere in the world has the priesthood been devoid of opportunism, especially for economic advantage and power. What we remain content to elicit from the relationship of the Yoruba priesthood to both natural and man-engineered phenomena, and his very existence is simply the ethos of responsiveness, of a lifetime of community integral dedication, a complete immersion in the ancient principles of their calling to that extent that they cannot divest their religious calling from social responsibilities, as captured in the very attributes of the Orisa. The babalawo is the wistful embodiment of all that is missing in the political life of a continent.

Need one remark that Ifa is not without its own tendency toward self-promotion? We are speaking after all of a profoundly humanized construct with all mortal flaws and ambiguities, even contradictions—and so we find that Ifa is also filled with verses that speak of the headstrong and of cynics who merely fall deeper and deeper into misfortunes, until they return to the original path already mapped out by Orunmila, the divinity of Ifa. There is a crucial difference, however. Care is taken not to suggest that it is Orunmila or any agent of his who is responsible for their misfortunes—no—it is their ori, destiny, the portion that they brought with them into the world, that very definition of their being that Ifa did no more than diagnose before leaving them to their own devices, to their own choices. Nor is it, for instance, the rejected deity who proceeds to take up his or her own cause by assailing the luckless head of the unwilling acolyte—the gods remain totally indifferent toward who does or does not follow them or acknowledge their place in mortal decisions. The priest of Ifa never presumes to take up cudgels on behalf of the slighted deity. No excommunication is pronounced, a killing *fatwa* is unheard of. The language of apostasy is anathema in the land of the Orisa. There is neither paradise nor hell. There is no purgatory. You can neither seduce nor intimidate a true Orisa faithful with projections of a punitive or rewarding afterlife. What does Ifa recommend in this here and now? That is the question!

With such caveats, a periodic visitation to the world of the Yoruba—or indeed to any of the "invisible" world-views—should thus be deemed a contemporary spiritual inoculation for millions of Africans, including the non-Yoruba, non-Christian, and non-Moslem, as well as Christians and Moslems, for whom this will surely serve as a catalyst for a systematic assessment of their existing cultures, values, and social conduct, especially their relation to others. It is not necessarily the self-promoting theologies that hold the monopoly of truth, justice, or tolerance. Orisa, our convenient guide into the offerings of the invisible religions, is the voice, the very embodiment of tolerance. Not for one moment of course do we suggest that the faith that is Orisa claims monopoly on these virtues— on the contrary. We simply urge those who attempt to promote the intolerance of one religion on African soil, in modern African nations, through the route of proclaiming its *comparative* tolerance—real or imagined, provable or merely speculative—in relation to another alien faith, to be far less zealous in such a gratuitous exercise, and to recognize, to begin with, the demonstrable tolerance, both in act and in precepts, of the anterior world of any people. The Yoruba understanding of the nature of truth is indeed echoed by the Vedic texts from yet another ancient world, the Indian, which declares:

> Wise is the one who recognises that Truth is One and one
> only, but wiser still the one who accepts that Truth is called
> by many names, and approached from myriad routes.

Its equivalent will be encountered in the well-known pronouncement of
an African sage, known as the Sage of Bandiagara, of Mali:

> There exists your truth, there is my truth and there is—the
> Truth.

Tierno Bokar may have been a Moslem; he was, however, a philosopher
first, and he drew his wisdom from a long ancestry of African traditional
thought.

The accommodative spirit of the Yoruba gods remains the eternal
bequest to a world that is riven by the spirit of intolerance, of xenophobia and suspicion. This spirit of accommodation—if we may spend a
little more time on the nature of these gods—this habit of ecumenical
embrace is not limited to the domestic front or to internal social regula-
tions. The Foreign Affairs department—and that is not so whimsical a
designation in a career that has entailed, in such poignant and universal
dimensions, strategies for relating its material world to intruding spiritual zones and evolving a philosophy of cohabitation and survival—the
Foreign Affairs department has shown itself equally adaptable to the incursion of foreign experiences. To understand the instructional value of
this in relation to other religions, one has only to recollect that, for some
religions, even today, the interpretation of their scriptures in relation

to human inventiveness is toward foreclosure, so that modern innovations in the technological and cultural fields are simply never permitted. We may choose to call these fundamentalist sects, but authority for the exclusionist approach to new phenomena is always extracted from or attributed to their scriptures—the Bible, the Koran, or the Torah.

Yoruba spiritual accommodativeness, we continue to remind ourselves, is not unique to that part of the African world. The following, for instance, comes from the adventures of a South African individual in his search for a spiritual anchor, a search that was as much conditioned by political events as by an innate Orisa temperament, sanctified by the examples laid out in the very histories of the deities' own search for wisdom. My correspondent writes of her father's funeral:

> His burial was very dignified and beautiful. . . . It was clearly his day. He was celebrated, honoured and people spoke not of a saint but of a man of integrity, a leader (without any formal position) and counsel in his community. Of course, it would not have been my father's funeral if the community did not speak of his pride, strong will, self possession, dignity, humour, style, wisdom, outright obstinacy and eccentricity.
>
> He was after all, my grandfather's son, the guy who walked out of the Anglican Theology College and converted to Islam in the 1940s. Because he just could not put up with the arrogance and racism of the English missionaries and thus broke with a family tradition of Anglican priests. My grandfather lived with my grandma who was not interested in entertain-

ing this "nonsense" and so they were both fully practicing their religions without any interference. . . . He also trained through correspondence course and qualified as a certified homeopath. As a black homeopath, he could only get his medical supplies from overseas through a Mr. L . . . , a Jewish businessman and friend from Cape Town. He practiced in the little town of Korsten at the back of one of his Moslem brother's fish and chips shop. There was a curtained door with a discreet sign "Dr. M . . . P. . . . .—Homeopath." So, people of all races ducked into the fish and chips shop and went to see the homeopath.

Later, he was disillusioned with Islam and its internal contradictions, as he saw them, moved to Cape Town but kept friendship with his Moslem brothers. Eventually, [he] left Islam and trained as igqirha/sangoma and went back to the Anglican church. My grandfather, by the time he died, he was practicing sangoma, herbalist, poet and had the first black-owned car, a Buick, smoked and took pleasure irritating white shop owners in the "white only" entrance he would enter with his cigar. My father was very proud to see these defiant actions and always told us and my father would answer back "oh but Mr P. . . . , there must be an error. I see no sign that says smoking is not allowed." P. . . . could not argue because the few white missionaries who came in the shop were smoking away.

. . . He was immersed in the traditions and rituals of the Anglican church. A few months before he died, he woke to

the sound of the drum and at 2 am followed the direction of
the sound and found where izangoma had gathered. He did
a round of dance and simply sat back and listened and when
he'd had enough, he went back home and slept. The following day, wearing a cassock and surplice, preaching about
"the God of Justice and acceptance," he told the story of
his night wanderings. I suppose to him there was absolutely
nothing strange about this. The few orthodox and hardcore
Anglicans in the congregation realised that this was "u-Oupa
ngqo, for real" and kept their mouths shut. . . . . . ja,
ngowamútata lowo, that's my father.

"Ewe ngu Ifa lowo nguye ngqo, yindlela nemisebenzi yakhe. Yintoni
into enganziwa ngumntu?—that's the way of Ifa, Ifa which, in its mysterious way, made me recipient of the letter on the death of a kindred
Yoruba spirit, a sangoma—from which the above is excerpted—even at
the very moment of writing of this deity! The corpus of Ifa, which we
may consider the closest to any aggregation of spiritual findings and
urgings of the Yoruba that go by the name of scriptures or catechism—
Ifa emphasizes for us the perpetual elasticity of knowledge. Ifa's tenets
are governed by a frank acknowledgment of the fact that the definition of truth is a goal that is constantly being sought by humanity, that
existence itself is a passage to Ultimate Truth, and that claimants to
possession of the definitiveness of knowledge are, in fact, the greatest
obstacles to the attainment of truth. Acceptance of the elastic nature of
knowledge remains Ifa's abiding virtue, a lesson that is implanted in the
Yoruba mind by the infinitely expansible nature of the gods themselves.

Is it any surprise that in Orisa religion, the concept of infallibility in doctrinal matters, or Revelation as the last word, does not exist?

Thus, even the gods evolve. Examine the attributes of Sango, for instance—what was this deity at the time of his adoption by Yoruba society? The god of lightning. Following from this principle, Sango's portfolio becomes extended to include a scientific discovery and application—electricity. Michael Faraday was not born in the land of the Yoruba, and certainly the autochthones of that land were not aware of the fact that he was the first to succeed in establishing the nature of electricity by harnessing lightning charges through a kite and running them down to a receptor. Nevertheless, when electricity came to the Yoruba, it was immediately added to the portfolio of this god Sango.

We must stress that the relation between humanity and gods is not hierarchical but of mutual exchange. The understanding of the nature of existence is thus one of complementarity, an osmotic relationship in which states of consciousness, transformed or influenced by progressive knowledge, flow into one another, taking from and giving back, replenishing the universal store of vitality from which consciousness takes form and motion. Faraday encroaches on a preexisting force of nature that was embodied in Sango, and Sango's being, in turn, is enlarged by the scientific extension of human ingenuity. In such a conceptual universe, how can the gods themselves fail to remain earthed, evolving even as transcending?

How do the Yoruba apprehend this material as well as essentialist relationship, integrating it into daily consciousness and ensuring that it re-

mains pertinent to secular designs? It may help to imagine three spheres—
not hermetic but fluid, more like whorls of gaseous emanations. One
represents the world of the Ancestor, another the world of the Living,
and the third the world of the Unborn. Whirling around all three is
the transitional vortex of creative energies which form the habitation of
gods and demiurges. The Living, the Unborn, or the Ancestor, passing
from one sphere of existence to another—a process that we call transfor-
mative awareness, principally through birth and death—partially dissi-
pate their vitality into this transitional space, replenishing its primordial
energies. That flux, that whirlpool of transitional force, constitutes the
Yoruba definition of universal consciousness.

The question of afterlife naturally looms large in all religions,
death being such a milestone of a truly profound metaphysical provocation. The difference with the Yoruba world-view—shared with a number
of other African peoples—is that the Yoruba experience this otherworld-
liness as a palpable, vital reality that is interwoven with the present.
The world of the ancestor—or afterlife—remains perpetually an affec-
tive consciousness among the living. The ancestors are integrated into
the present, not merely through the formal mechanisms of seasonal
celebrations or festivals, such as our already encountered ancestral masquerades, known as *egungun;* they can also be invoked through rituals,
incantations, or through a symbolic transference of ancestor presence to
a newborn child by the deliberate act of naming. We are speaking here
of the conscious retention of absences—thus, when you encounter a
child called Babatunde or Iyetunde—meaning, the father or mother has
returned—you understand immediately that a departed member of that

family line has been "reinstated" among the living through a child that was born sometime after that family's bereavement. In these, and in a number of other ways, the world of the ancestor, the world of the living, and the world of the unborn are woven together in mundane, domestic consciousness. This is a very different concept—let us make the distinction—from ancestor worship. There is no domestic pantheon among the Yoruba, so there is no automatic elevation to the status of deities just because you have joined the ancestors.

In the process of their visitations, the gods assume form, shape, and character—and responsibilities. They acquire supervisory roles over phenomena, in some cases becoming thoroughly identified with them. Thus Oya, Osun with rivers; Esu with the crossroads, chance, the random factor; Sopona, diseases; Sango, lightning; Ogun, metallurgy and the lyric arts, etc. A similarity in structure with the Greek pantheon has provided the subject of more than a shelfload of doctoral theses.

Let us spend a little time with that last mentioned—Ogun—confessedly my adopted companion principle. Mythological deductions indicate that the deities themselves appear to experience a need, periodically at least, to be united with the mortal essence, no matter the excuse—altruistic, self-sacrificial, in pursuit of mortal redemption, or simply as an adventure in divine tourism. What is ascertainable in nearly all the myths of the gods is that they do not seem to be able to keep away from humanity. For the Yoruba this craving merely betrays a sense of incompletion, however transitory—an interpretation that serves as a profound earthing device, ensuring that the deities do not exist as remote projections in ether. This craving led to the epic journey of the gods in their search for the world of mortals, a need to re-humanize themselves.

Alas, as they attempted to set out, they discovered that aeons of time had blocked their way. The passage back to the habitation of mortals had become overgrown and impenetrable. One after the other the deities tried to find a way, but each time they were beaten back.

It was then that Ogun came to the rescue. We have already encountered him from time to time, but here is the rest of his C.V.: god of all metals, protector of the forge, custodian of the sacred oath, and embodiment of the lyric arts. The mastery of iron and the evolution of metallurgy are of course crucial phases in human development—far older and more basic to culture than the entrapment of electricity—hence the especial notation that is given to the iron age as a quantum leap in the progression of culture. There is no question that the formal investment of Ogun in Yoruba consciousness is coterminous with a phase in the discovery and development of metal. Ogun was the deity who forged the primal instrument that hacked through primordial chaos, blazing a path for the gods' reunion with man. Ogun submitted himself to be ripped apart in cosmic winds, reintegrating his individuality through the sheer exercise of will power, the mystic tool in his hands. His equivalent in Greek mythology is obvious—Prometheus. Ogun's myth, however, operates on a level beyond myth making. So significant is the Yoruba assessment of the discovery of metals—a dramatic advance in technological evolution—that nothing less than the co-option of the entire Yoruba world of deities, and their relationship with mortal beings, could bear the full weight of Ogun's epiphany. It went even further. It was as if, encountering the virtues of metallic ore, its paradoxical character of durability and malleability, its symbolism and utility as alloy, the Yoruba read in it the explication of the potential integration of disparate elements of all nature and human phenomena.

The gods—it is pertinent to emphasize—are products of a primordial unity, as narrated in the myth of Atunda—literally rendered as "the one who recreates." Atunda is the shadowy figure of the Orisa pantheon, but his one act was truly revolutionary. Through circumstances that remain equally ill-defined, he shattered the original godhead into what we may now read as a principle of one-in-plurality and plurality-in-one. So now, beset by a yearning to unite with that portion of their original essence that had been flung across primordial void, a vital shard of an original unity that became the primogenitor of mortals, they decided to undertake the perilous journey across the void. In other narratives we encounter a version in which the supreme deity, Orisa-nla, had created the world of mortals, left them to their devices, and then one day invited his fellow deities to accompany him on a visit to see how that world was faring. No matter how it is slanted, the constant element is that the gods desired to return to the earth they knew, desired to be reunited, desired a recapture of their missing essence of an original unity of which humanity was a part.

My suspicion is that this is a corruption of the original myth, and that it smacks too much of the Christian myth in which the supreme deity descends to earth in the body of his son, gets killed, and thereby atones for the sins of the world. Like those other world religions, Christianity and Islam—the former from pagan Asian myths, the latter in turn from its elder sibling, Christianity—Ifa is not averse to some creative plagiarism. Also, as we discover in the Yoruba strategies of cultural survival in the Americas, accommodating Christian and other supremacist interventions within an ancient world-view was part and parcel of the armory of the culture itself. No matter what version of these myths we choose to adopt, however, there is unanimity in the narrative that Ogun plunged into the seething chaos and extracted from within it the only element that would guarantee its defeat. That element was iron ore, and from it Ogun forged the mystic tool, then wielded it to hack a path for other gods to follow. It was this feat that earned Ogun a place as one of the seven principal deities of the Yoruba pantheon, and one to whom belongs the pioneering urge—one of his praise songs goes thus: "He who goes forth where other gods have turned."

On arriving in the land of the mortals, all the deities, like our well-endowed tourists, went their different ways, each encountering a different adventure. Ogun ended up at the town of Ire, where the people adopted him as theirs and, intuitively, crowned him king. Then came war. Yielding to the people's importuning, he led them into battle. At the very height of victory, his sight clouded by an overindulgence in palm wine, he slew foe and friend alike. When his vision cleared he grieved, abandoned his throne, and retreated into the hills where he continued to mourn his day of tragic error, cultivating a farm patch and converting his terrible discovery to peaceful use.

Do we see here why the Yoruba would in no way be overexcited by the moral lessons of the horrors of, followed by the peaceful conversion of, atomic energy? Today Ogun is guardian deity of all workers in metal—the truck driver, the engineer, the airplane pilot or astronaut. All human adventure is prefigured—symbolically, not as textual dictation—in the history of the Yoruba deities. Thus, there is no surprise, no inhibition created from scientific encounters, no impurity in their digestive system. Some new phenomenon, friendly or hostile, is encountered, and from within the armory of Ifa and the accommodative narratives of the gods, an understanding is extracted. Even more crucial for the harmonization of mortal society, an ethical principle has been inserted here—and this applies to nearly all the deities: even the gods must express remorse for infractions, and make restitution. Only then can they be rehabilitated and society undergo healing. The annual festival of Ogun features this fatal dereliction of Ogun in a procession of remorse. Perfection is denied the deities, including Obatala, the paradigm of saintly virtues.

We begin to understand now why it was so logical that the Yoruba deities should have survived in the New World, across the Atlantic, while most other religions and cultures from the African continent atrophied and died. Adaptation is always easier in multiple guises, and in a spirit of the quest. Encountering the Roman Catholic saints in the worship of their intolerant masters, these slaves, who were already steeped in the universality of phenomena, saw the saints as no more than elective channels and symbols of the spiritual quest, and repository of glimmerings of Ultimate Truth. They were intercessors to supreme godhead, bridges between the Living, the Unborn, and the Ancestor world. If the plantation masters were hostile to any implantation of African spirituality on the soil of the Indies and the Americas, the solution was handy—co-opt the Roman Catholic deities into the service of Yoruba deities, then genuflect before them. Yes, the slaves in Brazil, Cuba, and other South American locations did bow to alien gods, but the liturgies that they intoned were very much the liturgies of their authentic spirituality.

The process went much further; it moved beyond internalization of spiritual allegiance and embarked on an appropriation of the Christian symbols, and this, unquestionably, was in response to the insistence of the slavemasters that their slaves display visible signs of their conversion, that they mount the iconic presence of the saints even within their paltry domestic spaces, their "cages." So the slaves displayed the images of the saints but addressed them in the parallel names of their own deities—St. Lazarus/Sopona, St. Anthony/Ogun, Our Lady of the Candles/Osun, Baron Samedi/Esu. And here is the lesson: this never constituted a spiritual dilemma, since the system of the gods has always been one of complementarities, affinities, and expansion—but of the nonaggressive kind. The deities could subsume themselves within these alien personages and eventually take them over. One cinematic illustration suggests itself—those films of alien body snatchers where the creatures from outer space insert their beings into the carapace of earthlings, eventually dominate, not only the human forms but the environment and culture, insert themselves into crevices of landscape and social actualities and can only be flushed out with the aid of weed-killers, flame-throwers, gamma rays, or quicklime. The difference of course is that the African deities were made of sterner yet more malleable stuff—the principle of alloys. Always generous in encounters with alien "earthlings," they accommodated, blended, and eventually overcame.

This was the outcome of the encounter, despite the passivity of Orisa. Orisa do not proselytize. They are content to be, or considered not to be. We need not embrace the Orisa, however, to profit from the profound wisdoms that can be extracted from the Ifa. Our repositories of exclusive spiritual truths can learn from this ancient, unassuming faith of our forebears. Ifa is tolerance. Ifa takes issue with any religion or faith that denies tolerance a place in its worship. Ifa embodies the principle of the constant, spiritual quest, one to which the notion of apostasy is unthinkable. How could it be otherwise when the source of knowledge, Orunmila, the mouthpiece of the supreme deity who directs the feet of the seeker toward a spiritual mentor or guardian deity, is not granted the status of infallibility even within Ifa, the very source of his wisdom. The Supreme Orisa, or ultimate godhead—Orisa-nla, also known as Olodumare—is nothing like the Christians' "jealous god," but the Orisa are nonetheless the true embodiment of that Christian dictum: Seek and ye shall find.

Religions that lay claim to world stature on certificates of ultimate truth and universality should pause and demand of themselves: Why is it that the worship of Orisa has never, in all these centuries, and even on hostile foreign soil, spawned an irredentist strain? The answer lies of course in the fundamental, accommodative intelligence of the Orisa. We need only contrast this with the catechism of submission that is the pillar of faith in other religions, such as Islam or Christianity.

It is evidently too late to eradicate that habit of reification of intuitions that equally answers the name of religion or superstition—depending on who is speaking, and of what practices—but we can at least determine how best to make them serve the cause of humanity, ennobling rather than enslaving the being that demonstrates the ability to bring the creations of his own intuitions to near palpable existence. Whenever we choose to abandon the sterile field of contestation between the existence and nonexistence of God, we can begin to concentrate instead on the question of how belief or nonbelief, and the structures that uphold either conviction, can assist the survival of those it most concerns—humanity, especially in the realm of ethical choices. Of these, tolerance is perhaps the most relevant, the most sorely in demand in our global dilemma. It is thus an appropriate note on which to end this section. Tolerance, in its own right, is at the heart of Ifa, a virtue worth cultivating as a foundational principle of humanistic faith—the catechism of the secular deities, a spirit of accommodativeness that is powerfully captured in the following odu, the IKADI, from the pronouncement of Ifa:

> B'omode ba nsawo ogboju, bi o ba ko ogbo awo lona, kio o
> gba a l'oju. Bi o ba ko agba isegun, ki o je e n'iya lopolopo.
> Bi o ba burinburin ti o ri agba alufa nibiti o nfi ori k'ale, ki
> o d'oju re de 'be. A da a f'awon alaigboran tii wipe: Ko si
> eniti o le mu won. Ee ti ri? Eyin ko mo pe: Ajepe aiye ko
> si f'omo ti o na ogbo awo. Atelepe ko wa fun awon ti nna
> agba isegun. Omo ti nna agba alufa nibi ti o gbe nkirun, iku
> ara re lo nwa. Warawara ma ni iku idin, warawara.

Ifa says:

> Aggression attuned, the brash youth meets a veteran babalawo and strikes him in the face. He meets an old herbalist and subjects him to torment. He runs into a venerable

Moslem priest bowing in prayer and rubs his face in the ground. Ifa divined for such insolent ones who boasted that they were beyond correction—is that so indeed? Don't you know that enjoyment of earth's plenitude is denied a youth who strikes a servant of Ifa? Premature is the death of the youth who strikes the devout imam at his devotions. Speedily comes the death of maggots, speedily.

Let us bear in mind that Islam—like its elder sibling, Christianity—invaded the black world, subverted its traditions and religions, often violently and contemptuously. It rivaled the earlier aggressor violence for violence, disdain for disdain, enslavement for enslavement. Both of them proven iconoclasts, yet what wisdom does this largely defamed and near-invisible religion of the Orisa prescribe for its own adherents? Tolerance, it enjoins, tolerance! You humiliate the Moslem or indeed any religious cleric, warns Ifa, and you will die the death of maggots.

We know we shall end up as food for maggots, but to also die the death of maggots? Now that is one fate that is truly worse than death. May Orisa-nla protect us all from such a fate—*A-a-Se!*

To recapitulate: Sources of conflict between nations and among peoples exist in the struggle for economic or natural resources as much as in the tendency toward the tyrannical temper of ideas, be these secular or theological. For the latter, the problem does not really lie with Christianity or with Islam, Judaism, or Hinduism, etc., but with the irredentist strain that appears to have afflicted these world religions, unlike the order of the Orisa. We need to remove the veil over these invisible religions and ask again: Why is it that the Orisa has never, in all these centuries, spawned an irredentist strain? Orisa separates the regulation of community from spirit communion even while maintaining a mythological structure that weaves together both the living community and the unseen world. But that world of the spirit does not assume any competitive posture whatsoever over the pragmatic claims of the real world. *B'enia ko si, imale ko le e wa.* If humanity were not, the deities would not be. And very much in the same frame of apportionment is the seeming paradox that, while every mortal is believed to have brought his own *ori,* or portion, destiny, into the world, that same view of existence declares: *Owo ara eni l'a fi ntun t'ara eni se* (With our own hands do we redirect our destiny). Volition, not submission, sums it up. Humanity, not deity, is the begetter of metaphysics.

The final word must be an admonition to the theocratic politicians who are resolved to set the continent on fire, and it is urgently directed at those meddlesome closet clerics of the intellectual tribe who provide pretentious, spuriously objectivized academic covering fire for the incursion of prejudice, creating smokescreens to divert our attention from issues of life and death, issues of human dignity, mutual tolerance, and mutual respect. Our counter propositions arise as much from the glaring failures of the world-views they have chosen to promote as models of perfection, or as liberalized exemplars, as from our knowledge of the tolerance amplitude of religions and world-views that existed before the advent of these binary flag-bearers of religious imperialism.

Between fanaticism and community, Orisa elects community. Orisa *is* community. Community is the basic unit, the common denominator, the glue of human society—this is the lesson of the Orisa. And in the strategies for regulating and preserving community, the Orisa have ceded the right of choice to humanity, and to the deductions of its intelligence—accepting the role of, but not subjected to intuitions and their interpretations, even by the most enlightened priesthood. Even the collective manifestation of faith, the breeding ground of fanaticism, witting or unwitting—church, mosque, temple, or shrine—is membership restricted and excluding by attestation, unlike the secular order, community, which by definition embraces all—this, Ifa advocates, and it defines its universe of conviction. Religion, or profession of faith, cannot serve as the common ground for human coexistence except of course by the adoption of coercion as a principle and, thus, the manifestation of its corollary—hypocrisy—an outward conformism that is dictated by fear, by a desire for preferment, or indeed, the need for physical survival. In the end, the product is conflict, and the destruction of cultures. Let this be understood by the champions of theocracies where religion and ideology meet and embrace. Orisa admonishes them: you will not bring the world even close to the edge of combustion. The essence of Orisa is the antithesis of tyranny, bigotry, and dictatorship—what greater gift than this respect, this spirit of accommodation, can humanity demand from the world of the spirit?

Thus, for all seekers after the peace and security of true community, and the space of serenity that enables the quest after truth, pleading for understanding from the Orisa for this transgression of their timeless scorn of proselytizing, we urge yet again the simple path that was traveled from the soil of the Yoruba across the African landmass to contiguous nations, across the hostile oceans to the edge of the world in the Americas—*Go to the Orisa, learn from the Orisa, and be wise.*

8. Thus Spake Orunmila: Africa as Arbitrating Voice

AND NOW, WITHOUT FURTHER ADO, let us seize upon an immediate, dominant issue from within the cultural divisions of the world, upon which we can call on the collective wisdom of the Orisa for arbitration, seeking guidance of our feet toward the beginning of mortal wisdom. It is essential to stress that we make no claims to absolutes in our interpretations of Orisa precepts but exercise the same confident measure of righteousness with which Moslems, Christians, Buddhists, etc., endow their scriptural derivatives. Let Orunmila guide us on the vexed discourse of rights and relativity.

The religious polarization of the world is manifested in numerous forms of unjust conduct that profit from prejudice, opportunism, and will to dominate. A reminder: two halves of the same monotheistic belief structure appear locked in an ironic, arrogant contestation. Ironic? Arrogant? Yes, because in their global contests, both sides of a binary conditioning fail to recognize, or take into reckoning, the existing claims of other groupings as interested or concerned parties, or as participants in the human search for truth and wisdom. Such victims of relegation are of course bearers, additionally, of the consequences of their fall-out, united though the twin remain in the implicit nullification of other forms of beliefs and world-views. It is a level of arrogance that is doubly ironic, since the total population of the non-Christian, non-Islamic worlds surely exceeds the sum of both, not counting those among them who are only nominal followers of either religion and routinely take out spiritual insurance policies by observances that are clearly neither Christian or Islamic.

The gods do not descend from their remote perches to take part in arguments that allegedly derive from their will—except, of course, in mythologies, of which the Greeks and Hindu are the most notorious, though the most considerate, since they carry such incursions into the world of theater and thus temper divine pronouncements with poetry, catharsis, and even riveting visual contrivances. It is the human agents who claim to receive, enshrine, and enforce their pronouncements. Let this be borne in mind as, without any claims to divine revelation, we proceed to interpose what we, followers or mere students of Orisa, propose as extracts from their mysteries, liturgies, histories, and myths, insisting yet again on no immutable truths beyond what other mortals just as close to, or distant from, their deities claim as derivative absolutes—be they named seers, bishops, mullahs, saints, ayatollahs, supreme pontiffs, etc.—and promote as encyclicals, fatwas, hadiths, commandments, etc. We shall pass over their methods of enforcement as being avoidably prejudicial, especially when contrasted to Orisa's understated methodology of peaceful demonstration and exegesis.

In an article commissioned by *Granta* journal on the significance of the first black president of the United States, Barack Obama, I gave some attention to what might be called his "foreign inaugural speech," delivered in Cairo. My view of the address—in common with millions of others, surely—was that it was timely and courageous, a sorely needed reaching out to a people and their cultures, toward which a perceived ingrained hostility and disrespect by the western world had not only soured relations but undermined the prospects of global security. Even the most cynical would concede that Obama's speech opened a passage toward the realization of that elusive but always potential peaceful collaboration among races, cultures, beliefs, and traditions, and that it challenged habitual, adversarial thinking and positioning on numerous levels. However, it was also a disturbing speech in one crucial aspect— the rights of humanity, and the doctrine of relativity of cultures that we sometimes encounter among cultural proponents. Here are some pertinent extracts:

> That speech . . . however, constitutes its own peril, capable
> of breeding an all too ready accommodation with contest-
> able aspects of such traditions, and the opportunism of their
> proponents. Nowhere is such a danger more likely than in
> the case of a leader who is determined to end the dismal record
> of a nation that attempted so arrogantly to be, not only the
> world's policeman, but its political moralist. The gesture
> towards conciliation, within the rubric of a respect for the
> traditions and usages of other lands, other societies, is of
> course unexceptionable. However, the world has numerous,

and interlocking constituencies, well outside those of nation boundaries, and when a constituency in question accounts for no less than fifty percent of the world's population—its women—there is great need for circumspection.

The right of women to veil or not veil, is not in question, indeed, is not the question, the question being whether or not any practice is transparently founded on choice, or imposition. The veil is, in addition, even beyond its function as a physical act of separatism, a metaphor for much else that is actual, some of which involves consequences predicated on freedom and enslavement, life and death, and thus impinges on the province of human rights, volition and dignity. We are living in a world, sections of which unfortunately take pride in perpetuating traditions of sectarian control, marginalization and dehumanization, traditions that are maintained only through the denial of choice to their citizens, where indeed members of an internal "lower constituency" are harassed, publicly lashed, imprisoned, stoned to death—sometimes for showing an inch or two of flesh beyond the eye-slits graciously permitted for the practical purposes of motion. It would have been preferable that Obama had either avoided the veil as sign of his affirmation of the right to cultural differences—a different issue from cultural relativity—or else proceeded to make a determination also on issues of personal choice and group compulsion.

Profound issues such as the existential condition of women

in society—any society—deserve more than a point of view dictated by only one "tradition," most especially when there are also available contradicting traditions within that same Tradition—with capital letters. Within Islam, the Talibanic view of women is a far call from the Moroccan or Algerian, the Indonesian from the Iranian, and so on. Even within tradition with a small "t," there exist further minuscule fragmentations. These evolve as society itself develops in ways outside its immediate cultural context—such as trade or technological encounters. Why, we may ask, does Saudi Arabia—but not other Islamic nations—still prevent her women from driving motor vehicles, yet mobilized them for that very purpose during the Gulf war, only to re-impose that status after the war was over?

Above such incidents of usage loom considerations of the basic attributes of man or woman. The jihadists of Somalia have lately introduced drastic punishment for any man or woman who shakes hands with someone of the opposite sex—assuming of course that they still have hands to deploy for such an immoral activity, the rulers having taken to public amputations of hands and feet as punishment for petty theft, a habit that stigmatizes, by association, even victims of abnormal circumstances—war, accidents, disease etc. In any case, this form of punishment calls into question the very act of permanently disfiguring a human being for one infraction or the other. In the case of the veil and womanhood, its evocation, being an aggressive symbol of subjugation—in multiple guises—cannot help but expand the parameters of its cultural significations and consequences for a section of humanity.

Once evoked, the ramifications of such a symbol as the veil fall within the realm of legitimate discourse. The undeniable, globally manifested actuality of differences within even so-called traditions calls attention to a large variety of options in interpretations and practices, even within supposedly hermetic theologies. That gesture of moral relief to the endangered species within societies of inequality was an avoidable omission in a context that was, after all, of Obama's own instigation. Sadly, it was left to President Sarkozy of France to seize, within that same week, the high ground of egalitarian morality, as he bluntly voiced his detestation of the "degradation" of women through sartorial confinement.

In precolonial Nigeria, among the Igbo, as readers of Chinua Achebe's *Things Fall Apart* will recollect, twins were considered a sign of evil and were thrown into the evil bush. By contrast, just next door among the Yoruba, twins were and are still venerated. They are in fact considered minor deities in their own right, and wooden figurines called *ibeji*—a favorite collectors' item for art lovers, prominent in foreign galleries—were carved in order to earth them in the present as it were, since they are considered rather temperamental, and one or both might decide to return to their world of the Unborn. Whenever one twin died in infancy its carved figure would be preserved and cherished, treated to a symbolic morsel of whatever its surviving partner enjoyed on earth. It would be washed, painted in camwood, oiled, clothed, and taken to ceremonial events, usually tied by a sash to the back of the mother or the surviving twin if a girl, just as if it were a living child. Well, the loss of twins to the Igbo in those days was the gain of the early Christian missionaries. They were quick off the mark to the homes of any "unfortunate" bearer of twins and took the babies in charge. They made forays into the evil bush, picked up the abandoned "monsters" and nursed them back to life, turning them into their first-line evangelists for the conversion of others.

Needless to say, that "tradition"—with the mentality that bred it—has been near totally abandoned, but the mentality that breeds the culture of stigmatization is not wholly eradicated—and we do not refer to the Igbo alone, nor should these remarks be restricted to Nigeria. In a certain part of Northern Ghana, for instance, there is a tradition that dooms the young women of a village "brides of the gods" in perpetuity. Not to put a gloss on the matter, they are designated domestic, farm, and sex slaves, to be supplied on demand by the village to the priests of a revered shrine. I made a reference to that practice in a lecture in Accra only five years ago, citing the practice in the past tense, only to be informed at question time that, despite the government's efforts to eradicate the practice, it was still prevalent in that same part of Ghana. To my astonishment, I learned also that even very recently, the practice received robust endorsement by an intellectual and poet who questioned the right of the government to intervene in matters that were part and parcel of a people's tradition. Tradition also sustains the routine stigmatization of the Untouchables as a cultural given in contemporary India, despite the fact that, thanks to progressive thinking, strenuous educational campaigns, and government resolve, an Untouchable now sits as a member of the Indian parliament.

The Nigerian equivalent of the Untouchable, the *osu* caste, is still upheld in certain parts of the East. Similarly, what a vast population of the world would consider horror killing translates as honor killing among some extreme sects, not only in Islamic outposts but among other Asian, non-Moslem families. A number of such incidents—or failed attempts—have been recorded within the United Kingdom in the first decade of this millennium, one of which involved the participation of an entire family. For refusing to marry a designated husband and persisting in carrying on her affair with her chosen lover, the unfortunate daughter was found guilty of bringing shame and dishonor to the family, lured into a trap, and decapitated by a brother.

The veil, this time quite literally, also manifests itself even in the unavoidable function of eating and drinking. As recently as the year 2010, in Abuja, capital of Nigeria, I witnessed a scene from which I appear to have been miraculously shielded all my life. The venue was the restaurant of Sheraton Hotel. That lunchtime, in company of my daughter and son-in-law, a diplomat, I watched a totally encased human form, in the company of her husband and three children, execute certain motions that could only be translated as a lunchtime activity. With the left hand she lifted her facial flap an inch or two and passed a forkload or spoonful of food beneath it. Since the piece of cutlery reemerged empty while the flap settled smoothly back in position, her routine could only be interpreted as feeding. At the same table, husband (unquestionably) and children ate and drank like the rest of the clientele. Was she suffering, I wondered aloud, from a communicable disease, or was this in conformity with some cultural usage? If the latter, how binding and universal was this specific usage even within the cultural milieu—clearly of Islamic definition—and where would its authority be found? How did the rest of the Islamic family, the Nigerian branches included, look upon it? As an expression of pure form of faith immersion? Or as a deformity? Would the Yoruba, for instance, regard this as a violation of that essence of religious tuning—no matter what religion—that is captured in the expression—*Gba were m'esin?*[1]

Cultural relativism or respect is therefore not the talismanic mantra for the resolution of the human predicament—indeed, it is only the beginning of a complex, ethically rigorous exercise, not its terminus. It is especially demanding because it requires a readiness for the interrogation of absolutes—not merely for the culture under scrutiny but for the scrutinizing side which, even without so declaring, has already positioned itself on legitimate critical grounds, often presumed higher. The very phenomenon of power and its exertion over others is very much part of the discourse, and it assists in clarifying one's position to a large extent, power being a craving that sometimes manifests itself in a need to impose conformity, to dictate, or to intrude in matters of choice that stress the singularity of the human entity. Even mythology is co-opted,

1. Madness in piety's embrace.

as in, for example, the imposition of taboos, and by mythology I do include the scriptures of any land or faith.

I should make a clarification: we are not yet engaged on the territory of the right of external intervention. The problem indeed is that very often, the two issues—the claims of tradition of which one happens to disapprove and the right of others to intervene—become confused in arguments, even as mere speculative propositions. They are often deliberately conflated, so that the right of intervention and the assigned motives for intervention override all possibilities of subjecting—as dispassionately as possible—the claims of this or that tradition to a valid scrutiny. We can take a shortcut and install the dimension of the fundamental right to life as the foundation on which all other rights are based, arguing for the abandonment of any social act that undermines that right or degrades the quality of that life, the right to which is obviously fundamental. This is one useful direction, but one that can be undermined through the evocation of extreme scenarios where the continued existence of an individual is proven to endanger the chances of survival of the total community.

With quality of existence we find ourselves on even shakier ground, since this provokes subjectivity. We may argue, for instance, that the facial cicatrix does not necessarily degrade the quality of an individual life, since we know that, in my part of the world at least, there are cicatrized individuals who have risen to the very top of the social ladder, are professionally fulfilled, well married, and not socially stigmatized in any way. Thus, those microcultures that still impose this form of disfiguration on children are not guilty of a breach of fundamental human rights. This might be reassuring for our seizure of responsibilities as we determine choices for children. Eventually, however, we encounter the adult who, despite social success, is traumatized each time he looks in the mirror or socializes. We are thus moved into the wider territory of traditions whose consequences are irreversible, extending into an age that is generally agreed to be an age of choice—which surely must come however late, since no tradition on earth can prevent it. Sooner or later the child proves "the father of the man," but now, that man considers himself permanently disfigured, and society has encroached on that portion of his or her existence which the very society has designated the age of volition. Obviously this adult has been shortchanged in life, and the choice that was denied him as a child proves a defect of social usage.

Society is thus obliged to protect the adult in formation, which in turn requires intervention on behalf of what we designate as the age of innocence, vulnerability, or social impotence. And if the life of a child is made a misery by his or her peers owing to the mark of *difference* which, as we shall have cause to develop as we proceed, may prove a handicap to the developing entity, and a danger to society, then again we have to consider the possibility that such traditions cannot be dismissed as being relative but must undergo other tests, even internal, such as: Does such a practice serve community interest either in the present or the future, seeing that society itself does not stand still? Or does it constitute a time bomb ticking away at the security of society? A trauma inflicted in one's childhood, we know, may warp a child's character or social development. We know, for instance, what permanent damage is done physiologically to the girl-child subjected to female circumcision, or whom tradition surrenders to men for premature copulation.

It is therefore possible to consider arguments advanced by society for dictating or overriding the choices of its own members, either as individuals or as group entities—in short, the restricting norms of the overall society for its efficient functioning or as strategies for survival, even where this is by no more than a control elite. It is within that narrow provenance that relativism can claim rational consideration, not even automatic approbation but at least the right of consideration: the rights of the individual against the right of communal survival. Outside of this evocation, one that must be grounded on actuality, not speculations, we need not expend much argument over how the forces of law or the community should react in Ogun state of Nigeria if an indigene from another part of the nation, resident in Ogun, decided to toss some newborn twins over Olumo Rock, or an immigrant family decapitated the daughter of the house for wearing her skirt above the knee and applying lipstick to her face, all in the name of cultural relativism.

On that basis, then, let us return to President Nicolas Sarkozy of France, who declared, quite bluntly, that he found the burqua degrading. This form of dress, which covers the woman from head to toe, leaving only slits for the eyes, is a form of imprisonment, he said, isolating women from society, and he called in his address of June 2009 for legislation against it. Another point of view, which we shall reserve for another place, is that the burqua is in fact a statement not so much about the status of women but about the insecurity of the male sex in such societies. African males, however, take their masculinity for granted, just as women do their femininity. This may explain why traditional African society cannot conceive of women shrouded from head to toe, especially under the burning tropical sun!

France, as it happens, supplies the Orisa with quite a generous selection of policy enforcements for adjudication in her self-appointed role of global *agent provocateur* on issues of culture and human dignity. Under Sarkozy's predecessor, Jacques Chirac, a social eruption occurred in the educational sector when his minister—obviously carrying out government policy—banned overt religious symbols in the attire of pupils on school premises. It generated heated debates, for and against, both within and outside France. For several nations this was not just an abstract debate but an urgent real-life issue, over which governments other than France had weighed options in response to their social concerns, and the need to balance what they saw as the safety of the totality against the choices of one or more of its constituent elements. Those choices were not neutral. Even if intended as such, that is, restricted to the basic right of choice, whenever such choices are not unrelated to a specific history they cannot be considered neutral. The policy edict by Chirac's government was definitely related to the escalation of religion-inspired terrorism that France had undergone internally some years before, and by which the nation still felt threatened. The need to curb the spread of such destabilizing tendencies was hardly open to debate. We can, however, argue—as earlier conceded—for or against a specific strategy of containment.

Unfortunately, this in itself often becomes a one-sided debate, since, as we all know only too well, governments have a convenient wall behind which they retreat—national security! Those of us outside that wall, however, are still left with the interrogation of the parameters within which such decisions are taken, expanding the debate into the very principles from which society takes shape, such as—in the case of an educational environment—society's responsibilities to its vulnerable sector—youth—and the shaping of its personality in a way that does not conflict with the survival or collective rights of society. The frustrating aspect of such debates is that they are nearly always conducted along the already stated binary lines, one side assumed to hold the values of a Christian west, the other of the Islamic east. Other cultures and their usages are hardly ever looked upon as being relevant to the implications of such discourse—perhaps they are considered to have evolved in uninhabited spaces or else habitations without a record of mores and traditions of their own.

It is easy to simplify the debate—as was done at the time—by evoking the nature of club membership. A public school has certain rules, and if you wish to be a member, or make use of its facilities, then you must conform to those rules or seek accommodation elsewhere. This merely begs the question. In any case, the world we inhabit has changed vastly and dramatically over the past few decades, and club rules—like race- or sex-differentiated membership rules in social clubs—are no longer as sacrosanct as they used to be. The law courts are open in some societies, and legal procedures and judgments render further arguments moot. Despite such remedies, however, the genie is still out of the bottle, and the beasts of intolerance, suspicion, and polarization merely relocate or transmute, continuing to stalk the streets in some place or the other. Having learned to mutate, developing resistant strains, they become correspondingly intolerant and contemptuous of that poor relation—dialogue or logic—substituting terror and intimidation.

Ultimately, one can most confidently take up positions that are, ironically, relative, subjecting one's experience in the present to what one has known in the past, admitting dispositions that have shaped one through the years, in addition to a knowledge of what obtains over the walls of other places, compared to which the culture in question is seen as either an aberration or a rational and/or humanistic course.

The *problematique* lies at the heart of that mantra—"cultural respect"—as a righteous absolute in itself. Did Chirac's move against ostentatious religious attire and ornamentation in schools offend such an absolute? Or did it in fact question its very claims to existence? It helps to seek answers outside Europe and, where else? In Africa. We shall again resort to that nation, Nigeria, one that finds itself in recent times routinely faced with the sectional evocation of the absolutist mantra in an increasingly deleterious manner that expresses itself in the violent deaths of hundreds, and openly questions the very right of society to exist on its present terms—cohabitation of a plurality of faiths, traditions, and social practices.

This episode took place some thirty years ago, that is, long before the introduction of the sharia—Islamic law—by one state, soon to be imitated by a handful of others, albeit still a minority. Until that dramatic turn in the religious politics of Nigeria, religion, beyond the fact that it was practiced, was virtually a nonissue, though admittedly prone to sporadic clashes between adherents of the rival faiths—Christianity and Islam in the main—with traditional worship such as the Orisa being occasionally served up as a sacrificial appetizer.

After several decades of independence, during which the issue

of school uniforms in public schools never emerged as a social problem, the nation was startled out of her complacency when a minister
of education acted in a direction that was the very opposite of Jacques
Chirac's—he ordered that secondary school pupils be made to dress in
distinct fashions dictated by their religious belonging. It would appear
that this education minister, a Moslem, had woken up to the revelation
that the uniforms worn by pupils in the various secondary schools—the
shirt/blouse, shorts/skirts, with or without shoes—were "Christian" and
thus discriminatory against non-Christian pupils. This order was received with little enthusiasm, and several of his fellow Moslems expressed deep skepticism about the move. The minister lost that battle
but could rightly claim that he did launch a war. Let us now take a
look at Africa's pre-Islamic, pre-Christian ethos in such matters, and
see if it is possible to draw some conclusions from them and even bring
their lessons to bear on this yet unresolved global issue, albeit with clear
indications by some European governments that have established their
position through legislative action or declarations of intent.

It is possible to propose that the fears of those who opposed that
minister's attempt have been borne out today in the deep religious cleav-
ages that have become the identifying character of parts of the nation,
divisions that have exacerbated over time and now manifest themselves
in religious clashes of ever-increasing savagery. One took place—or,
more accurately—resumed in Jos, Plateau state in Northern Nigeria toward the end of 2010, of such intense bloodletting that, at one stage, a
round-the-clock curfew was imposed and the military was brought in to
enforce some modicum of order, at least temporarily. Religious clashes

in that part of the country have reached epidemic proportions. If I may invoke the ultimate horror, about twenty years ago, gangs of butchers from the Islamic side of the religious divide invaded schools, separated the pupils of one religious faith from others, and slaughtered them while invoking a pious benediction on the process. Others will recall the rampage that ripped through the capital city, Abuja, allegedly in protest against the Miss World beauty contest, whose finals were to take place in that city. Such exhibitionism was against Islamic teachings, declared the promoters of the riots. Homes and businesses were destroyed and some two hundred lives lost in a day's rampage. A large number of these invaders were youths, known as the *almajiri,* schooled in the madrassas, ready brainwashed and unleashed by their mullahs—and political opportunists—against the rest of society. The statistics and frequency merely depress the mind—let us simply sum up current actuality with the lament that, in contrast to the harmonious cohabitation of diverse religious beliefs that I enjoyed as a child, all the way through secondary school and beyond, the reign of religious zealotry, enveloping and consuming entire communities, has become a way of life.

The basic question then, posed by the French and Nigerian experiences, among others, indeed an increasingly global question, is: What does the totality of society owe its younger generation—almajiri, boy scouts, girl guides, choir boys, or street hawkers—in a world that is so easily ripped apart by the manipulation of religious differences? Here is one answer from a traditional model.

The modern school is the equivalent of the age-grade culture in African societies, one which the supposedly advanced, sophisticated western societies, shaped by Freud and Kinsey, might do well to study. In the societies we speak of, the rites of passage from one phase of social existence to the next are bound by rules that eliminate exhibitionism, and these include the observance of strict dress (sometimes semi-nudity!) codes.[2] The purpose of such usage is to create a common group solidarity distinguished only by age and the identification of aptitudes, enabling the pupil to imbibe not only a formal education but a sense of place and responsibilities within the community. At the heart of this strategy is purposeful leveling. Thus, such traditions obliterate, in a child's life, a separatist sense of "the other," and each sees the other as a human equal. One would not go so far as to propose that Columbine and similar American school tragedies would have been prevented by the observance of such a code of training, but it is not too farfetched to suggest that its absence, in some form or another, adapted for the realities of modern existence—one must be at pains to emphasize this, the principle, not necessarily the form in which that principle is structured—is a contributory factor to America's crisis of juvenile delinquency of tragic dimensions.

Derivatives from such a tradition are limitless. In conditions therefore that involve a plurality of religious faiths, a common dress code is simply a medium of arbitration and a foundation block in youth forma-

2. This is extended, in some instances, to the initiation of the adult into a chieftaincy or kingship grade, a period spent in prolonged seclusion under conditions of social leveling or status reduction. The intent is to immerse the initiate in the general condition of the society over which he is now expected to preside or play a leadership role.

tion, which, in turn, is the foundation block of society. Having observed alternative models in practice, I find the model of such upbringing infinitely preferable to most others. This proposes that, while the right of religious worship, even in schools, must remain sacrosanct—pending that stage of human development when religion is relegated to its rightful proportions as the exoticization of the irrational—society profits in the long run from muting the overt manifestation of religious separatism in places of public education. It is only in such a context, not from any notion of absolutes or the ready formula of religious binarism—one versus one other—that one can comfortably consider the interventionist order of Chirac. We may find that some religious augmentation of a school's dress code is not obtrusive, while others violently blare forth, intrude, provoke, and, most importantly, separate. It becomes difficult to fault a policy of creating the maximum possible sense of oneness in the process of youth formation. Allowance having been made for differences on those days allocated to spiritual exercises of choice, no harm, objectively speaking, is done to the young mind when it is thereafter bound, with others, in a routine expression of a common identity, and that includes, most prominently, the school uniform.

This formula extends to nonreligious choices, providing a strong argument against the "liberal" school of thought that despises a dress code, this being considered a constriction of self-expression in youth. It enables us to view religion, though of contemporary catastrophic prominence, as not the fundamental issue but—*difference*—the structuring and near-deification of difference as a principle of upbringing, which of course is where the seeds of later problems are sown. What this supposed notion of enlightened education has meant is that children from affluent homes can attend school in outfits that range from designer elegance to deliberate slouch baggies, which signal exclusive associations distinguished by an elitist consciousness either of moneyed or gangland aristocracy, in contrast to impoverished farmers' and workers' children, who can just about scrape together the odd pieces of castoff dressing from charity or second-hand clothing markets. A simplistic reading of the rights of the young, which are not in dispute as principled—that is, a humanity at a yet impressionable age—the translation of such rights into unbridled self-expression—another debating point of cultural contrasts—is responsible for the takeover of learning environments by fashion parades and the breeding of the exclusionist ethos based on class privilege. If one believes that youth should be weaned away from any sense of social superiority through a display of sartorial affluence in school, it seems only logical that the even more penetrating demonstration of religious elitism should be equally discouraged. "I am wealthier than you," as an attitude among youth, earns our general disapprobation. No less an institutional responsibility toward an impressionable age grade should be the attenuation of all buntings that, today especially, leave impressionable youth with the message "I am holier than thou."

Thus, to touch briefly on Nigeria's contribution to international terrorism of the religious brand, if one were to award degrees of culpability to that product, Abdulmutallab, who tried to blow up a passenger plane over Detroit, a substantial amount of responsibility for the foundations of such extremist conditioning that calcifies the mind would go to preachers and practitioners of the gospel of separation wherever found, soul companions of that Nigerian minister of education. The French have an expression whose truthfulness applies to heaven knows how many unrecorded events in human history: the flap of a butterfly's wings results in a thunderstorm a thousand miles away. I would add to that—and a hundred years later, even a thousand.

Acceleration of the tempo of the negative in global relations is, most sadly, traceable to the contestation of cultures, but most especially of religion-based cultures. It hardly leaves room for a structured, routinely articulated examination of social principles between affected nations, much less an objective apprehension of what society itself means across cultures and faiths. What we are left with, recent year after year, has been how to manage the consequences that follow a failure to generate that debate, and across national divisions. In place of such comprehensive dialogue, nations resort to sporadic declarations, generated by increasing impatience with what appear evident excesses of one culture or another, their encroachments on the rights of others.

Alas—and herein lies the problem—in wide swathes of the world, such matters are not even open to discussion, are ruled out of bounds of normal discourse to mere mortal beings. The Dutch filmmaker Theo van Gogh was deemed deserving of terminal censorship for the crime of using the film medium to generate the debate, focusing on that gender that is compelled to bear the separation of the veil. He met his end at the hands of one such defender of the faith on the streets of Amsterdam. "The veil sucks," Salman Rushdie declared, though it could be claimed that Rushdie's position was predictable. However, we should note in passing that a highly respected Islamic scholar, Adil Salahi, at the al-

Furqan Islamic Heritage Foundation in London joined a number of other Islamic voices in declaring that there is no basis in the Koran for the veil. "Cultural respect" therefore continues to beg the question of whose culture? Is its geography physical—a marked space—or does it translate in the human—wherever such humans are placed? How is it defined? And how much of a righteous absolute can it truthfully be deemed?

This of course still leaves open numerous aspects of the right to personal choice, once we have extracted the lesson that, even within cultures that claim to be monolithic, there are both material differences and subtleties of doctrine. There will be found other Moslems who agree with Adil Salahi, while others would like to burn him, not simply in effigy but in full corporeality. For writers and advocates of cultural rights whose constituencies lie outside the main rivaling and dogmatic binary entities, each such eruption merely provides us the opportunity to insert that missing text, the potentially corrective text of the missing (invisible) cultures. There is a need to depolarize these combatants, to remind the protagonists of the religiocultural wars that the world does not spin on the vertical or horizontal axis of their oppositional views. There are other world-views, other structures of cultural usage that robustly manifest their viability not only on the African continent but in the Americas and in the Caribbean—in Cuba, Brazil, Colombia, Puerto Rico, etc.—I refer of course to the Orisa world of the Yoruba.

What are the pronouncements of these and other anterior cultures—such as the Hindu, Buddhist, Confucian, or Yoruba—on the subject of the veil-allied agencies of separatism? The Yoruba summarize it in one sentence: *Oju l'oro wa* (Communication lives in the human face). Thus Speaks Orunmila. As volunteer spokesman, confessedly biased against the imposition of absolutes, I continue to stress the arbitrating authority of these alternative worlds and the failure of embattled cultures to profit from their attributes—most especially their nonhegemonic virtue—articulated in myth and scriptures as vibrantly as in living practices. We now propose a change of scene that takes us through another field of cultural relativism—this time of the much-ignored relativism of *responses* to the *phenomenon of culture,* even among proponents of one and the same culture. We proceed to Germany, home to Moslem Turks in large numbers, to address a five-year-old incident.

To set the scene, fleshing out the event to which reference was made in the Preface, we shall access some direct media reports on that cultural episode in the contest of "cultural respect." They provide a balanced account of the positions and moods of those whom the controversy most concerned. The extracts also save the trouble of reminding us, as we must continue to recollect, that the incident did not take place in a vacuum—very much the contrary. Conveniently, the reporting both catches the tempo, and places the event in the context of global happenings around cultural practices, religion, and allied sensibilities that have pursued the world into this millennium. Here now are the narrative extracts from the international media—the *New York Times, Le Monde,* and *Die Welt,* among others.

The Deutsche Oper in West Berlin announced on Monday it was replacing four performances of "Idomeneo" scheduled for November with "The Marriage of Figaro" and "La Traviata."

The decision was taken after Berlin security officials warned that putting on the opera as planned would present an "incalculable security risk" for the establishment.

In the production, directed by Hans Neuenfels, King Idomeneo is shown staggering on stage next to the severed heads of Buddha, Jesus, Poseidon and the Prophet Mohammad, which sit on chairs.

Two weeks ago Pope Benedict sparked outrage in the Muslim world by quoting, in a speech in Germany, from a medieval text linking the spread of the Islamic faith to violence.

Last year, the publication of cartoons of the Prophet Mohammad in a Danish newspaper sparked violent Muslim protests around the world.

German politicians denounced the opera house's move, deputy parliamentary speaker Wolfgang Thierse saying it highlighted a new threat to free artistic expression in Germany.

"Has it come so far that we must limit artistic expression?" he told Reuters. "What will be next?"

Peter Ramsauer, head of the Bavarian Christian Social Union (CSU) in parliament, said the move pointed to a "naked fear of violence" and called it an act of "pure cowardice."

Interior Minister Wolfgang Schaeuble also criticized the decision. "We tend to become crazy if we start to forbid Mozart operas being played. We will not accept it," he told a news conference during a visit to Washington. . . .

The director of the Deutsche Oper, Kirsten Harms, defended her decision at a news conference on Tuesday. She said Ehrhart Koerting, Berlin's top police official, had phoned her in mid-August and warned her of dire consequences if the opera house proceeded with its plan to show "Idomeneo." "If I had paid no attention and something had happened, everyone would rightly say that I had ignored the warnings," Harms said.

Koerting issued a statement confirming the conversation, but saying the decision to cancel "Idomeneo" had been Harms's alone. Police have said their concern was prompted by an anonymous phone call in June but they had no evidence of a specific threat. The Deutsche Oper decision precedes a much-hyped meeting on Wednesday between Schaueble and representatives of the country's Muslim community to discuss ways to improve dialogue and integration.

The above excerpts provide the global setting, amply outlined. And now to the reaction of marginalized cultures, those "invisible religions" that the world continues to ignore as possible sources of cultural arbitration.

Buddha, Jesus, Poseidon, Mohammed . . . when I viewed the roll call of this decapitated company, I must confess that my hands itched to decapitate the director—no, not of the Deutsche Oper, Kirstin Harms, but of the opera itself, Hans Neuenfels. Where, yet again, I demanded, was the Yoruba world in all this? Ignored as usual, by the Greco-Asia-Arabo-Eurocentric director! Where was evidence of the much-vaunted rhetoric of multiculturalism? Not one African deity, not even as mere tokenism! To these artistes, Africa does not exist, much less matter. If ever there was an opportunity to display the heads of the Yoruba Orisa—Sango, Ogun, Oya, Sopona, and the rest of the Yoruba deities on an egalitarian platform, *Idomeneo* was a most accommodating vehicle, and the director fluffed it! Had he never heard of affirmative action? It was an opportunity to bring the African, and especially the Yoruba, into operatic ecumenism, entitled to all rights and artistic privileges, to iconization, veneration, and creative deconstruction on a par with others.

I can already hear the question—would the traditional devotees of these Orisa of the Yoruba world not find such theatrical decapitation of their deities offensive? Decidedly not. And let us meet head-on the ready comment that this is the mere claim of a westernized sophisticate, indoctrinated and alienated by the cynical and irreverent ideologies of the west. Quite plausible, but if such voices first studied the nature of the god Esu, from the Yoruba pantheon, and the principle of demystification, the rejection of afflatus in life becomes lodged where it rightfully belongs. But the explication is also lodged in history. The world of the Orisa has been accustomed, is still accustomed—as already amply narrated—to the disdain, the contempt, and the blasphemous conduct of the worlds of Christianity and Islam for over two thousand years. Thus, quite obviously, their bodiless heads would do nothing but smile at the thought that any further derogation of their status was still conceivable, or could draw blood among their followers, especially for being paraded in a sumptuous production, complete with special lighting, a symphony orchestra, chorus, and prima donnas. They are more accustomed—those who escaped the fury of religious arsonists of both persuasions—to being served up at museums and art galleries, exchanged at cutthroat prices from collectors seeking some kind of gratification that has no bearing on their authentic essences or spiritual significations. Centuries of decontextualization and misrepresentation have inured them to any outlandish settings such as the operatic. If anything, they would be delighted to find themselves sharing a centuries-old experience of manipulation with the deities and avatars of other lands.

There is, however, an even more fundamental proposition. Since we are unable to guarantee the purity of motivations of this opera director, we can only speculate, giving full rein to the operations of the creative imagination as guaranteed by the world-view of the major absentee deities on the operatic stage, conclusions that are rooted not merely in immediate actualities of the world as we live it, but also on the deductions of history through the conduct of the so-called civilized worlds from the Inquisition to jihadism, and their tenacious, tyrannizing theological constructs.

So, let us imagine a film or theater director from my world of the Yoruba seeking an artistic statement that could adequately convey the desecration of humanity, and the constant invocation of gods and goddesses as authorities for such desecration. Such a director is seeking a metaphor to shock either national or world conscience into an appreciation of what is done in the name of religion, sets out to indict supposed men and women of culture of the crime of deicide. What more effective image can one conjure than to go one up on Salome and serve up the heads of Christ, Mohammed, Buddha, Shiva, and company on wooden platters? Is the director's message, in effect—this is what you have done to your deities and their avatars—God, Allah, Jehovah, Zeus, and all—you kill and mutilate them every day! I must stress that we are yet again deprived of knowing in just what manner the director of *Idomeneo* co-opted the presences of the gods and prophets, disembodied. Was he asking who, in the end, are the real deicides? Who really killed God? Who kills him, her daily? Indeed, who is it that is ready to kill over the question of whether or not the invisible deity is a he or she and whether he or she is dressed in blouse and trousers, in a burqua, or in a Scottish kilt and sporran? Is it those who desecrate childhood, who conscript children as soldiers, offer them communion, tie a cross or a *tesuba* around their necks, and send them into battle, co-opting the name and image of God for the elimination of his creation? Or is it the theater director who shocks us with interrogatory images?

What we witness daily, in other words, what rips apart our humanity, from the supposedly "smart bombs" of the United States and Israel that pulverize innocents and militants alike, to the suicide bombers of Iraq, Mumbai, and lately Nigeria, and the boasts of twenty thousand Hezbollah rockets poised for a rain of fire on civilians, all in the name of faith—albeit with economic and territorial complications in places—to the genocidaires of Rwanda where no names of any deity were directly evoked but whose religious prelates were hyperactive in the massacres—

all these are nonetheless negations of claims to the spiritual aspirations of man, his nobility of spirit, and it is naïve for one to think that, given these realities, the sanctity of the supervising icons of faiths—as long as the faithful continue to invoke their authority—will not be challenged, graphically and symbolically. Visit the sessions of the International Courts for Crimes Against Humanity and pursue the role of the Christian priests who not only participated in the killings of Tutsis and those deemed sympathizers, but actually directed the operations. In the already cited instance, the shepherd of the flock lured the sheep into his church as guaranteed sanctuary, only to summon the *interehamwe,* the Hutu killing squad, to where the lamb had been penned for easy slaughter. In Nigeria, the year 2009 was ushered in with killings that left over five hundred dead, many in the most gruesome manner, disemboweled, bits and pieces of the victims stuck on stakes and paraded through the town. The subsequent years have been no less assiduous in religious savagery, the year 2011 topping all previous records in the orgy of pietistic homicide.

Well then, what was the ultimate fate of *Idomeneo?* The cancellation was effected. It led to resignations and public protest and eventual political intervention. A series of meetings ensued between the directors of the Deutsche Oper, the Town Council and its police, and the Moslem community. I met the leadership of that community by chance, introduced to them in 2008, in Bayreuth, where they had attended a public event in my honor. I had made a reference to the cancellation of the opera in my acceptance speech. The Moslem community revealed that they had made no protest, that they had had no hand whatsoever in the decision to cancel performances for an opera none of its members had seen. The performances had in fact been rescheduled, and the program eventually took place, exactly in its intended form and without incident. Clearly these were children of Orisa, self-confidently embedded within the Turko-German Islamic community.

We must not be sanguine, however. This particular episode could have ended in the opera director, the nation's president, and the chancellor being burned in effigy, while far-flung zealots would seek to outclass the piety of their resident protesters by decapitating real-life innocents and earn themselves preferment in the rewards of afterlife. Where deities are co-opted to lend authority to human sentiments or proclivities, humanity becomes disposable to usurpers of divine authority and custodians of mere dogma. One's mind goes back again and again to the title and subject of a film by the French cineaste Jean Rouch. That title is *Les Dieux Meurent Aussi* (The Gods Also Die), shot over fifty years ago, a work of great sensitivity that successfully penetrates through to the social significance of the spirituality of much of African religions. It is a film that underscores the community philosophy of the majority of what we have termed the invisible religions, the Yoruba among them. When that metaphor of divine mortality is fulfilled in the minds of the community of mortals, perhaps the much sought-after harmonization of a world of multiple faiths, even as preservers of enchanting tales, will finally be realized.

For now, to veil or not to veil is not the question. Volition or Imposition, Power or Freedom may yet prove the pervasive question of the twenty-first century.[3] And there, hopefully, Africa will not be content with the role of the perpetual victim of alien binaries. At the moment, the continent is thrust into limelight as the latest frontier of that conflict in a new Scramble for Africa—this time for her soul, but not yet as potential haven for the howling lost souls of her erstwhile denigrators—that wisdom is yet to come. Even more optimistically, in the process of that scramble, hidden values will also be unveiled, values that will confer on her an unaccustomed status—the vital role of a Global Cultural Recourse and—Arbiter.

3. On various fora, a view that has been expressed again and again for years before the commencement of the Arab people's uprising.